ON THE SOLDIER'S PATH

ON THE SOLDIER'S PATH

THE **WAY** OF **WARRIOR**

Based on The Five Spheres by Miyamoto Musashi

THAM TRONG MA

ON THE SOLDIER'S PATH
Tham Trong Ma

All rights reserved
First Edition, 2022
© Tham Trong Ma, 2022

No part of this publication may be reproduced, or stored in a retrieval system, or transmitted in any form by means of electronic, mechanical, photocopying or otherwise, without prior written permission from the author.

Paperback ISBN: 978-1-954891-48-7
Ebook ISBN: 978-1-954891-47-0

CONTENTS

Introduction 1

Part I The Five Spheres 5

Chapter One
Earth 7

Chapter Two
Water 23

Chapter Three
Fire 45

Chapter Four
Wind 75

Chapter Five
The Void 89

Part II Winning Wars Without Combat 99

Chapter Six
An Alternative Approach 101

Chapter Seven
Military Strategy 115

Chapter Eight
The Warrior and the Ethics of Warfare 145

Conclusion 165

Notes 167

INTRODUCTION

Dear Soldier,

For the love of country: This was your motivation when you set out on this journey, donned your uniform, and picked up your gun. You were not deterred by the rigorous training nor the fact that you would be separated from those you love most of the time. In our current world, peace has become a scarce resource, so you need to understand how valuable you are.

A country is a slice of humanity. Therefore, the moment you decided and followed through on becoming a soldier, you became a vital thread stitching a semblance of peace into humanity's fabric of chaos. It may seem that you are unseen, unknown, and unsung but always know that your blood and sweat are indelible imprints. And the earth—humanity—will never forget.

Only a few understand and appreciate the depth of your vocation. Even some soldiers get into the military for the wrong reasons. There are those who join because of the paycheck and benefits of being in the armed forces. Some join because it is a family tradition. Others want the prestige and respect that come with wearing a military uniform. Such reasons have made many soldiers stray from the true path of dedication and service. But just like everything else in the world, deviating from the true path is not new. And this is why I want to tell you the story of Miyamoto Musashi.

Miyamoto Musashi was a Japanese warrior who lived between the 16th and 17th centuries. Born on March 12, 1584, in Miyamoto-Sanomo village, Harima province, Japan, Miyamoto was respected as a *Kensei*—a sword saint of Japan because between when he was 13 and 29 years old, he fought in more than sixty to-the-death sword fights and was never defeated.

His fame spread through Japan when at 21, he defeated three instructors of a renowned swordsman school. In that fight, it was recorded that he fought against sixty opponents simultaneously, all armed with swords, muskets, spears, bows, and arrows. After that, he traveled and had one-on-one duels with many masters.

When he turned 30, he determined to train himself to gain deeper principles of swordsmanship. He practiced hard until the age of 50, when he discovered the Way of the Warrior and applied it to everything he did without needing a teacher.

Like what we see today, Musashi knew that many warriors stray from the true path of martial arts; thus, he decided to do two things: He founded a school of swordsmanship called Hyōhō Niten Ichi-ryū; and wrote books on the principles of swordsmanship he had gained. Musashi did these things to achieve one goal: steer the warrior's mind back to the true way. His most famous book, *The Five Spheres*, taught the principles and strategic significance of martial art based on his own principles. And it is on the foundation of Musashi's principles that this book, *On The Soldier's Path*, is birthed.

Miyamoto Musashi, who died on June 13, 1645, at the age of 61, may be long gone, but the principles of his martial art are relevant in the modern world. It is not surprising that Musashi's voice still resonates till today because if he could win more than sixty fights where his life was on the line, he definitely did many things right.

His ideas are simple yet laced with depth. They are like calm waters that run deep. For Musashi, a true warrior must master the Way of Strategy. This Way, practical and straightforward in its approach, is founded on one notion: defeat the enemy. Musashi teaches that defeating the enemy goes beyond fighting against the enemy's weapon; the true warrior must understand the enemy's psychology and circumstances and strategically employ them to his favor.

The book, *The Five Spheres* is a discourse on the Way of Strategy sectioned into five scrolls: Earth, Water, Fire, Wind, and Emptiness. In the Earth or Ground scroll, Musashi compares the Way to carpentry. Just like a carpenter who follows a plan to build a house, the warrior must also be methodical in fighting the enemy. The scroll also emphasizes timing and the importance of perception. The Water scroll is a guide to sword fighting. It teaches the warrior the right stance and gaze when facing an adversary. The Fire scroll deals with actual strategy—how the warrior can gain advantage and exploit the adversary's weaknesses. In the Wind scroll, Musashi criticizes the techniques of other schools of swordsmanship. Finally, he summarizes his principles with the Emptiness scroll or the Scroll of the Void, which lives a striking lesson: the more knowledge we gain, the more we realize how little we know.

For this book, *On The Soldier's Path*, these five scrolls are metaphors for the characters a soldier should possess. Just like Musashi taught, defeating the enemy is more about psychology and circumstances than engaging the enemy's weapon. The world we live in has seen many battles, all in a bid to resolve lingering conflicts. But the many wars the world has seen should show that the real enemy is not the next individual or the neighboring nation; the real enemy is our selfish individual interests that distract us from seeking peace.

Therefore, each chapter, each scroll in this book, will represent the different qualities a soldier can and should possess as he journeys on this long road to peace. Some of these qualities are opposites, but they make him complete when fused together in a soldier. Completeness is a crucial requirement for a soldier— because a broken soldier cannot restore order to a broken world.

So I consider myself, dear soldier, privileged to communicate Musashi's principles to you through this book. By reading this book and putting it to practice, the world will be a better place. This is the way I see it: I am leaning on the back of Musashi, while you are leaning on mine—and together we are gifting peace to the world. Our efforts are connected by different times and events and fused into a synergy for the world to enjoy a semblance of peace.

May this synergy never be in vain.

PART I
THE FIVE SPHERES

CHAPTER ONE

EARTH

Follow the Map

The earth holds a lot of significance for the soldier. The earth soaks up the blood and sweat of the soldier. The shrubs that sprout from the earth provide cover for the soldier to evade and target the enemy. Bunkers are dug under the earth. All the battles of a soldier are fought on the earth. Most importantly, on the earth lies the path or trail to the enemy.

The final destination of every battle is peace. So when you follow the earth's trail to the enemy's camp, the result after the battle will be peace. However, it would be myopic for the soldier to think that attaining peace *begins* and ends with strategizing, following the coordinates that lead to the enemy's quarters, and employing different weapons of war.

Musashi stated that in his Earth scroll, to know the immense and profound things, we must first understand the small and shallow things. What we see on the battleground—war cries, gunshots, bomb blasts, dead bodies—are the big things. But what escalates into war are the small things that are often neglected by the soldier. And if we lean on the words of Musashi, we can trace the path of peace down to the soldier.

There are two virtues for peace a soldier must possess. These virtues are like map coordinates—following or deviating from them can either restore or remove peace from the world.

Loyalty and Timing: The Soldier's Virtues for Peace

Loyalty

In Musashi's days, a samurai is known for carrying two swords—the long sword and the companion sword. The long sword is usually the weapon known as the *katana*[1]. This is the essential sword of the samurai. Asides from being used in combat, the katana sword symbolized the warrior's status and *unwavering loyalty* to his master.[2]

The companion sword, on the other hand, was usually the *wakizashi*[3]. Only samurais were allowed to carry the katana, but the wakizashi could be carried by anyone of the lower class. Because of its use in samurai suicides[4], the wakizashi was also referred to as an *"honor blade."* Samurais were never without their wakizashi. They carried it wherever they went and even hid it under their pillow while they slept. The samurai's wakizashi is likened to the pistol of the modern-day soldier.[5]

The pairing of the wakizashi and the katana is called a daisho, which literally translates to "big little." Daisho is not a weapon in itself but refers to the act of carrying two swords. Samurai warriors discovered that having two swords gave them a competitive edge during battle.[6]

ON THE SOLDIER'S PATH

So what does this mean for today's soldier? The katana and the wakizashi—or more aptly put, the daisho—represents loyalty. Beyond knowing how to wield a gun and throw a grenade, the soldier must have the primary virtue for peace: loyalty.

Loyalty is faithfulness or devotion to something or someone. All a loyal person thinks about is what or who they are devoted to. The circumstances around them do not matter so long as they protect the interests of what or who they are devoted to.

Just like the samurai carrying two weapons, loyalty for today's soldier is two-pronged. A soldier must be loyal to *humanity* and *country*. Loyalty to humanity is like carrying a katana, while loyalty to country is like carrying a wakizashi. Both are important, but in times of decision making, one becomes weightier than the other.

Remember, we have established that the soldier's path is one that leads to peace for his country and, ultimately, for humanity. So when he is faced with a tough decision, a soldier should ask himself: *How will this impact my country? How will this impact the human race?* Many disagreements have escalated into wars because people have failed to ask these questions and provide honest answers to them.

The world has experienced wars and crimes against humanity because people—soldiers—are neither loyal to country nor humanity, but to themselves alone. They project their self-centeredness on the rest of the world under the guise of fighting for their nation. But a close examination of the conflict's nuances would reveal that most (if not all) of the wars the earth has experienced would have been avoided if humanity was put first.

For example, World War 1, which lasted between 1914 and 1918, arose because of the competition for imperialist control. Serbia wanted to take over Austria-Hungary's control of the Slavic people of Bosnia and Herzegovina. This strong desire for control led to the assassination of Austria-Hungary's Franz Ferdinand, the Archduke of Austria. The assassination degenerated the conflict between Austria-Hungary and Serbia into a full-blown war that claimed over 17 million lives.[7]

Imperialist nations never clamor for the interests of the countries they want to dominate. The power tussle between Austria-Hungary and Serbia was a contest for increased wealth and dominance, and not for the good of the Slavic people of Bosnia and Herzegovina. When we say "imperialist nations," it is vital to bear in mind that a group of people governs a nation. Therefore, the fight for wealth and dominance was simply a fight for the pockets and pride of people who were ready to sacrifice human lives on the altar of selfishness, people who were only loyal to themselves and not to humanity.

Loyalty to Country: The Wakizashi
You are a soldier because you are defending your nation. Your primary duty is to your nation. Part of the United States Oath of Enlistment reads: ". . . that I will support and defend the Constitution of the United States against all enemies, foreign and domestic; that I will bear true faith and allegiance to the same. . ." So you ought to do what is in the best interest of the nation you serve and represent.

There have been many betrayal cases in military history where people have shown disloyalty to their country, handing it over to its enemies. For example, there was China's Qin Hui. In Chinese history, Qin Hui was a chancellor of the Song dynasty. He was a power-hungry fellow who removed all his political opponents and eventually handed the Song dynasty to the Jurchen dynasty. Another example is power-hungry Emilio Aguinaldo—a man who implored his nation, the Philippines, to surrender to Japanese invaders, with the hopes of getting the Japanese to make him the president of the nation. What about Mir Jafar, who received a bribe from the British East India Company and betrayed India to the British[8]; an action that led to Britain's imperialist rule over India for almost 200 years? The stories of Qin Hui, Emilio Aguinaldo, Mir Jafar, and every traitor in human history boils down to one fact: they were *only* loyal to their personal interests.

Peace is not only the absence of war or violence; it is also the presence of equality, equity, and cooperation. A soldier who shows disloyalty to his nation may not plunge the nation into war but would certainly remove vital aspects of peace like equality and equity. Therefore, as a soldier, you *must* understand that your duty to restore peace doesn't begin at the battlefield— it begins before then. It begins by wearing loyalty around your loins at all times like a wakizashi. When you maintain loyalty to your nation, the need to go into the battlefield may not arise.

Now, there is the question: If the primary duty of a soldier is to his nation, why is loyalty to country likened to the small wakizashi instead of the big katana?

Loyalty to Humanity: The Katana
Loyalty to country is great, but loyalty to humanity is greater. No individual or country exists in a vacuum. We are all connected and interdependent on one another. It is for this reason a soldier must holistically consider how his actions or inactions would impact not just his country, but also the world at large. Barack Obama understood this.

In his address to the nation on September 10, 2013, the then POTUS spoke about the Syrian civil war and the repressive actions of Bashar al-Assad, the president of Syria at the time who had killed over a thousand Syrians with poison gas, sarin. Except for being the world power, the United States actually had no business interfering with the affairs of Syria. As a matter of fact, many Americans either felt that the US had no business interfering, or that interference could escalate into a war, or that interference wasn't worth it. But that night, Obama underscored why the United States needed to attack Syria. His reasons were all founded on the need to respect and protect lives all over the world. He explained that the consequences of America's inaction and indifference could be far-reaching since "other tyrants will have no reason to think twice about acquiring poison gas, and using them."[9] He asked Americans to "reconcile [their] belief in freedom and dignity for all people with those images of children writhing in pain, and going still on a cold hospital floor. *For sometimes, resolutions and statements of condemnation are simply not enough.*"[10]

If we critically examine the Vietnam War, we will realize that the war would have been avoided if the conflicting parties,

North Vietnam and South Vietnam (and their allies), put humanity first before their competing ideologies. Both parties wanted a unified Vietnam but wanted to model the country differently. The North wanted communism, the South wanted a country with economic and cultural ties to the Western world.[11] If the belligerents had shoved aside their ideologies and put humanity first, then over 3 million people—of which more than half were Vietnamese civilians—wouldn't have died.[12]

There are times when the interest of humanity trumps the interest of your nation or personal interest. And as a soldier, you have to be rational to understand these times. Samurais did not carry their katana everywhere as they did with the wakizashi. The katana came into play in moments of the battle, in decisive moments. In the same way, you may not consider your loyalty to humanity in every situation.

In most cases, your loyalty to your country comes first. However, in critical moments when the human race is threatened, your decision must favor of humanity. Always bear this in mind, dear soldier.

Timing
Musashi said that there is timing in everything—from music to archery to riding horses. For a merchant, there is a time when his capital rises or falls. The same goes for a warrior; there is a time when he thrives and a time when he declines, a time of harmony and a time of discord. In every skill and ability, there is timing. And Musashi suggests that it is important for the warrior—the soldier—to understand timing.

Nations have successfully attacked other nations that did not understand the power of timing. Timing was all it took for Israel to defeat the United Arab Republic (Jordan, Syria, and Egypt) in what is commonly known as The Six-Day War, which lasted from June 5 to June 10, 1967. After the 1948 Arab-Israeli War, relations between Israel and its Arab neighbors didn't return to normal. Tensions kept mounting until it escalated in May 1967, and both sides started preparing for war.

The United States intelligence predicted that Israel had the capacity to launch a successful attack on the United Arab Republic with little or no warning. However, Israel never confirmed these predictions as the United States never knew the actual timing of the operation. The Israelis were discreet with their plans. They had robust security who did not reveal their plans or preparations. Apart from being discreet, Israel also played a multifaceted game of deception. First, they made Egypt believe that they would attack southern Sinai instead of the north if they were to attack. Second, they put specific measures to give the enemy the impression that an attack was not imminent. Some of these measures included: public statements by the then Defense Minister who told the world that Israel would rather go for dialog and diplomacy than launch an attack; issuance of leave to thousands of Israeli on the 3rd and 4th of June; and announcements that the Israeli government was only concerned with routine matters. The United Arab Republic relaxed. And on June 5, Israel successfully launched a series of airstrikes. What made Israel's attack even more interesting was that it was launched at an hour of the morning when most Egyptian officials were on their way to work and when the Egyptian Air Force chief took his routine daily morning flights.[13]

Reading about The Six-Day War, it is difficult to fathom how the United Arab Republic could be so careless. Who relaxes in time of hostilities? It was easy for Israel to deceive the Arabs because they made light of the time they were in. In a time of war, adequate preparations must be made. Nothing must be left to chance. Israel understood this, prepared, and won. In six days.

A similar scenario had even played out some years earlier during the Second World War. Hitler used a delay tactic to defeat Western Europe, which comprised Holland, Belgium, and France. The Central Intelligence Agency (CIA) noted that these three countries had "ample and repeated warnings," but since Hitler never executed the attack—having delayed for six months[14]—they took the warnings for granted. They even called it a "phony war" as Hitler postponed the attack 29 times, usually at the last minute. Before the actual attack, the countries had received information about it. However, the Dutch and the French didn't heed this warning, dismissing it as another false alarm. Only the Belgians were smart enough to place their forces on general alert.[15]

Just like the United Arab Republic, Western Europe downplayed the importance of timing. They went to sleep in a time of war. No matter how many times Hitler had postponed the attack, they should have been prepared, knowing that it was a time of war. The war had already lasted eight months, and its end was not even in sight, so why were they comfortable?

Israel and Germany had the same tactics: they made their enemy undervalue timing. They "infected" their enemy with a calm spirit, a spirit not prepared to fight. (This is a technique Musashi taught in the Fire scroll, and we will examine it later.)

Musashi rightly noted that there is timing in the whole life of a warrior. Therefore, your actions should be guided according to timing. One does not relax during a time of war; neither does one become hostile in a time of peace unless such a person is an enemy of peace.

As a soldier, every activity is encased in time. Musashi wrote the five scrolls on the basis of timing. But there is something I want you to know: every time should be a time of peace. The timing for peace should not be conditional. Everything should be done towards fostering peace. However, I do not neglect the fact that there would be situations that call for war, but before going to war, make sure it is the only option left.

I say this because many wars have been fought not because they were necessary, but because they were instigated by people who, ironically, "benefit" from the dividends of war. So dear soldier, when faced with a dilemma whether to escalate a conflict, ask yourself: *Is war necessary or do I want to fulfill a selfish goal?*

Through *The Five Spheres*, Miyamoto Musashi offered samurais a guide to true swordsmanship. Little did he know that his lessons would be a template for world peace more than three centuries later.

ON THE SOLDIER'S PATH

Musashi's Way of Strategy is absolute: kill the adversary. Peace ought to be absolute too, because *only* through peace would we thrive as individuals and collectively as a species. Unfortunately, just like many samurais did not follow the Way in Musashi's time, in today's world, peace in its totality is a mirage.

In teaching his Way, Musashi knew that it was not enough teaching samurais about (his) strategy or timing, he knew that samurais must first possess certain traits which would enable them become skillful swordsmen who understood timing. Today's soldier must also possess these traits—for if he does, the virtues for peace will come naturally to him. These traits include: honesty, understanding the Way of all professions, distinguishing the pros and cons in every matter, intuitive judgment and understanding for everything, recognizing the unseen, and paying attention to details.

- *Honesty*: This is a fundamental ingredient for loyalty. A dishonest soldier can neither be loyal to his country nor to humanity. He is never on the path of truth. The traitors we saw earlier were dishonest fellows who claimed to be true to their nation but later sold off their countries for selfish gains.

  Like Musashi, I am not just telling you to be loyal to your country and/or humanity, I am also letting you know that your loyalty is *dependent* on whether you are honest or not. So be honest with yourself and answer this: *Am I an honest person*?

- *Understanding the Way of all professions*: There are lessons to be learnt from other professions. There are a set of principles that guide every profession. Musashi even noted that asides the Way of the Warrior, there are three other Ways through which men pass through life; they can pass as farmers, merchants or artisans. The farmer understands changes in seasons, the merchant understands how to make profit, and the artisan is proficient in the use of his tools. The importance of understanding the way of other professions is to discover the similarities and differences between our way and that of other professions. Through these similarities and differences, we can pick vital lessons that will help us understand our own way better.

For example, a soldier should understand the way of medicine; the way of the doctor. The doctor is committed to restore health and life to the body. And he does this without considering political affiliations, race or religion. He is committed to only one purpose: saving lives. This leaves a lesson for a soldier, whose commitment should be to restore peace to a broken world and also protect lives.

Understanding the way of others is not limited to professions alone; the soldier should also understand the way, character, or ideologies of other human beings. As seen earlier, the Vietnam War occurred due to conflict in ideologies between the North and South. If the conflicting parties involved had understood that their way is not the only way, that the way of another may be more beneficial, then the war would have been averted.

Dear soldier, perspective is important. Hold on to your perspectives and ideologies because they form the ideals that guide you through life, but also be flexible enough to understand (and sometimes, accept) the perspectives of others. If not for your sake, at least for the sake of world peace.

- *Distinguishing the gains and losses in every matter*: Gains and losses are relative. What constitutes a gain for one person may be a loss for another. In fact, conflicts arise because parties clamor for what will profit them. Sometimes, there are situations that look like they have no gain, but by taking a closer look and looking at the big picture, you would see the benefits hidden like a pearl covered by dust. This brings to mind the story of Desmond Doss, a United States Army corporal.

Doss was the first conscientious objector to receive the Medal of Honor—the highest, most-prestigious personal military decoration awarded to military personnel who had distinguished themselves through their valiance. Why did Doss receive this recognition?

Desmond Doss served in the US Army as a combat medic. What made him an interesting character was his refusal to handle a rifle. His superiors and fellow soldiers, confounded by this decision, decided to persecute him. After several persecutions (including an arrest and a court-martial), Doss was allowed to serve as a combat medic.

In the Battle of Okinawa, Doss was assigned to the 77th infantry Division, which had the task of securing Hacksaw Ridge. In their first attempt to secure the Ridge, the Japanese launched a massive attack which drove the Americans off the Ridge. Now, instead of Doss to escape with his fellow compatriots, he returned to the Ridge to save wounded soldiers. For 12 hours, he single-handedly carried and lowered 75 soldiers from the Ridge. It gets more interesting as he also lowered wounded Japanese soldiers, although none survived at the end.

Logically, Doss's action was unwise. The American army had been overpowered by the Japanese, so there was no need to remain on the Ridge. No gain whatsoever. Staying on the Ridge was foolhardy. But Doss decided to look at the big picture. He knew that these wounded soldiers had families who they had promised a safe return from the war. He knew that the greatest gain is that which values human life. In that moment, as the smoke from explosions and the stench of decaying bodies rent the air, all Doss could think of was saving one more life. Without handling a rifle, Doss was able to restore hope to 75 people—and to everyone around the world that has heard this story. Doss's heroics validate my earlier assertion that a soldier's duty goes beyond strategy, coordinates, and weapons.

- *Intuitive judgment and understanding for everything*: The affairs of life do not exist at the surface. When you encounter a situation, you have to critically examine and understand it before arriving at a definite conclusion. Have a holistic view about everything—factor in the perspectives of others.

Dear soldier, before you pick up your weapon and go to war, carefully evaluate the situation. *Is the war necessary? What are the major causes of the conflict? Can these causes be addressed without escalating the issue into a full-blown war?*

There is a time for war, no doubt, but make sure you understand the situation and *honestly* come to the conclusion that war is the only option left.

- *Recognizing the unseen*: Intuition and understanding everything will help you see things that are not obvious to others. Sometimes, the gains or losses of a venture do not lie on the surface; you have to uncover the nuances to see what others don't see. Just like we saw with Desmond Doss, while others felt the wounded soldiers couldn't be rescued, Doss saw that there was hope for them. It didn't matter to Doss if these soldiers were maimed, all he wanted to do was to save their lives and give them a chance to reunite with their loved ones.

- *Pay attention to details*: This is the only way to recognize the unseen. You cannot afford to be careless as a soldier. Never dismiss anything as unimportant. In his book, *Atomic Habits*, James Clear narrated how the fate of British Cycling changed because they hired a coach who was keen on details. The coach broke down cycling into different processes and started improving on each process. He redesigned bike seats, hired a surgeon to teach the riders how to wash their hands to reduce their chances of catching cold, painted the inside of the team truck white so that specks of dust wouldn't go unnoticed. All these summed up to give British Cycling a well-deserved success.[16]

In a world where conflicts abound, where violence is the default resolution to conflict, it is easy to miss out the details that would birth lasting peace. But this is why you are different, dear soldier. You are a warrior, and you are not just one because of your valiance on the battlefield, you are one because you know the Way to peace. This is a knowledge many do not have. So while others only skim the surface in moments of conflict, you have to dig deeper, scrutinize, and see what others cannot see.

Dear soldier, set these principles to your heart. Master them. Let them guide everything you do. By applying these principles, you will get a broad perspective of issues and know how to handle them as a master of peace. Musashi wrote:

If you constantly pay attention to the Way and develop the culture of hard work, you will not only master your technique but also defeat your opponent.

Always remember that your opponent is not the next human being, but the systems that keep exploiting conflicts for gain. Contend against these systems. These systems are everywhere—from the racist police officer to the sexist filmmaker, the corrupt governor to the vile drug baron. If you can apply these principles and contend against these systems on a small scale, then you are bound to win on a large scale.

Key Point from Musashi: *In any given path, know how not to lose to others, know how to help yourself, and know how to build a reputation for yourself. This is the Way of the Warrior.*

CHAPTER TWO
WATER

Soft As Water

Many often think that a soldier should be one detached from his emotions. He should be stern and feared. He should only focus on war and the power he wields through his gun. Many soldiers have gone on to live according to this narrative, but this narrative is not a true definition of who a soldier should be. A soldier is like water. Water has the tangibility of solid and the fluidity of gas. Similarly, we seldom see soldiers but we know that they are working behind the scenes to keep the peace.

Water is unique. Flexible and assumes the shape of its container. Sometimes calm, sometimes turbulent especially when under the influence of pressure. Refreshing when calm; sweeps clean when turbulent.

In his Water scroll, Musashi, without directly stating it, used some of the attributes of water to guide the swordsmanship of the warrior. He outlined two main prerequisites for swordsmanship: Posture and Gaze. But before explaining these prerequisites, he taught warriors how to prepare their minds, and I have grouped his teachings into three striking points.

1. *In the Way of the Warrior, the mind should not be different from the spirit of your daily life. Let your mind be always calm and upright both in your normal life and in moments of battle. Do not change, not even a little. Do not be uptight, yet do not live recklessly. Be focused and keep your mind from wavering.*

What Musashi was saying in a nutshell is this: Let the soldier be calm . . . just like water. For the one who must bring peace must first be at peace with himself.

2. *While relaxing the mind from the environment, make sure the depth of your mind (your inner self) is strong. Do not allow others to influence your mind.*

During a storm, the sea experiences sustained winds. Waves come crashing down. There are loud, continuous crackles of thunder. But beneath the ocean there is total calmness. This is what Musashi wants for a warrior. A soldier should be able to maintain calm despite the disturbances he may face. Peace is not only the absence of disturbance, sometimes, it is the ability to remain calm amid the disturbance.

3. *Be open-minded. Look at things from a wide perspective, and in this vastness, cultivate wisdom.*

Your mind should be as vast as the sea. Stretch out. See the perspectives of others. Understand the way of others. Reflect deeply as you do this. Know that the path to peace sometimes lies in the unseen. So you have to collect different ideas, sift them, and produce what is in the best interest of humanity.

Posture

Musashi outlined guidelines for posture or stance a warrior should take during battle. But what does posture mean for today's soldier? It means how the soldier presents himself to the world. How does the world perceive him? A savior or a villain? Does his uniform instil fear, or is it a symbol of safety? What stance does the soldier take in social issues that plague the world? Is he on the side of truth and humanity, or is he a puppet of destruction?

Musashi's guidelines for posture can be accurately applied to today's world to put the soldier on the path of peace. Here are some of his instructions:

- *When you stand, your head should be straight, it should not tilt or droop or look up.*

This holds a literal meaning for a protégé of Musashi, but a figurative meaning for today's soldier. Uprightness is a fundamental requirement for the soldier. You must be morally upright. You must also be upright before the law. The fabric of peace is loosened at its seams by people who are not upright. And if you, as a soldier, must restore and keep peace, then you must also not be found wanting.

In the past, many soldiers have been found wanting in uprightness and that is why there is a long list of war crimes today. These crimes were not perpetrated by people or soldiers pressured by war, but by people who were already morally and ethically deficient. Some of the heinous war crimes committed in history[1] include:

- *The T4 Euthanasia Program*: In August 1939, physicians, nurses, and midwives received an order from the Reich Ministry to report infants under the age of three who appeared to suffer from severe mental or physical disabilities. Health workers suggested that parents send their children to certain pediatric clinics in Germany and Austria for treatment. On the surface this looked like a good plan, but the reality was that these children were not to be helped—but killed.

The T4 program, initiated by Adolf Hitler, gave physicians the power to determine which children were deserving of life. The Nazis justified the program saying that the funds used in treating these terminal illnesses could be channeled to "better" the lives of those who had no health condition.

Children were taken to these clinics and where put into gas chambers. Their dead bodies were disposed in ovens and their ashes placed in urns, which were sent back to their families alongside a falsified account of their death.

The T4 program ran for two years—from 1939 to 1941—and it was estimated by the U.S. Holocaust Museum that at least 5,000 physically and mentally disable German children were killed.

- *Unit 731*: The details of Unit 731 are even more horrific than those of Hitler's T4 program. Between 1937 and 1945, the Imperial Japanese Army carried out deadly experiments in northeast China. These experiments were carried out on human subjects, mostly Chinese and Russians.

The experiments, started by Lieutenant-General Ishii Shiro, were carried out by a group of 3,000 researchers known as Unit 731. Shiro hoped to use the knowledge of science to make Japan a world power. The aim of these experiments was to develop new treatments for the ailments that plagued the Japanese Army.

Shiro and his team vivisected prisoners without anesthesia; injected diseases such as syphilis, anthrax, and gonorrhea into subjects; and raped female subjects to carry out tests on their fetuses. They didn't stop there: they used prisoners as targets for grenades, burned people alive, and dropped plague-carrying fleas in Chinese villages to study how fast the disease spread. It is recorded that these horrendous experiments claimed between 3,000 and 250,000 lives in a single camp.

What makes the story even more chilling is that these researchers were never tried for war crimes. And here is why: The United States, in a bid to be ahead of the Soviet Union in global weaponry, chose to give these perpetrators immunity in exchange for the information gathered during the course of the experiments.[2]

- *Congo Wars*: Aside mass murders, one significant feature of the war in Congo (which lasted from the early 1990s to 2013) was mass rape. It is reported that the rape was so widespread and routine in Congo that the United Nations decided to class rape as an instrument of war, and not a side effect.

It is recorded that up to 1.8 million women in the Congo have been raped, averaging about 48 women per hour. And what is most shocking is that there is no age limit to the women targeted, as girls as young as 18 months old to women as old as 80 have been victims. In some cases, the genitalia of these women are mutilated, while their families are forced to watch.

In many cases, these women were ganged raped by 2 to 20 soldiers who took turns over and over again.[3]

- *Camp Sumter*: Georgia's Camp Sumter was meant to hold 10,000 prisoners, but Henry Wirz, the Confederate commander of Andersonville crammed 32,000 prisoners of the U. S. civil war into the facility.

Inmates were starved since food was scarce. Sanitation conditions were deplorable as prisoners had to drink the creek water filled with the fecal matter of diseased and dying men. As a result of these, many prisoners came down with scurvy, dysentery, and diarrhea. Prisoners who weren't killed by these diseases were killed by the poorly trained guards who shot inmates indiscriminately without cause. 900 prisoners died each month at the camp, and over 12,000 died between 1861 and 1865.

When Wirz was condemned to death for war crimes, he claimed he only followed orders.

These horrific tales of war crimes show the moral bankruptcy of many soldiers. A person who was not upright before joining the army can never be upright after joining the army. There is no valid reason to waste human lives. Before the horrors of Congo, the U. N. once considered rape a side effect of war, however, it is puzzling to think about why any soldier would want to rape women in the first place. Even without war, rape is already a crime, yet soldiers go ahead to rape innocent women who have already been emotionally and psychologically disturbed by the dynamics of war.

Musashi advised that the warrior's posture must be upright and should not droop, so dear soldier, have sound moral values and stick to them. Do not be influenced by other soldiers or circumstances around you. Henry Wirz, the commander at Camp Sumter claimed he was following the orders of his superiors. And I know this raises the question: *What should a soldier do when he receives orders from a superior?*

I wouldn't ignore the fact that this is a difficult question to answer since one of the golden rules of the military is "Obey before you complain." So should the soldier obey an order that ignores the sanctity of human life? Personally, I don't think so.

The army should not be too rigid in its workflow. Rules such as "obey before you complain" paint an inappropriate image of the army. An image of undue harshness, irrationality, and inability to listen to the voice of reason. When Musashi talked about posture or stance, he wasn't only referring to the posture a warrior should take during a duel, but also to how others— especially the adversary—see the warrior. How others see the warrior depends on how the warrior positions himself. Likewise, how the army, as a body, positions itself based on its rules and regulations, determines how civilians would see them.

The soldier has a license to wield any kind of weapon, but these weapons are not toys to be used anytime the soldier wills; they are actually instruments required to restore order and bring peace to a nation and/or the world. Guns are not more powerful or valuable than human life. So before answering the question, "What should a soldier do when he receives orders from a superior?" we must first understand and accept that rigid rules that seem to enthrone the soldier's will above human life should be done away with. When this is done, the soldier can now a follow some steps towards responding to orders.

I came up with an algorithm that can guide the soldier on what to do when he receives orders from a superior(s). This algorithm may or may not be feasible, but I believe that in a world where the rights and opinions of everyone is respected, these steps would go a long way to stymie gross misconducts and horrendous actions in the military.

The algorithm above shows the flow of steps a junior officer should take when given an order. The flowchart is self-explanatory, but I want to buttress on some steps. Remember: These steps were developed on the assumption that the "Obey before you complain" rule is not enforced.

When you try to reason with your superior and he still insists on going on with an action that threatens human life, you have two options: either you carry out that action, or you resign from the army.

—You can decide to carry out the order because you don't want to disobey your superior, but would you be able to live with the guilt that you carried out an order that antagonizes the sanctity of human life.

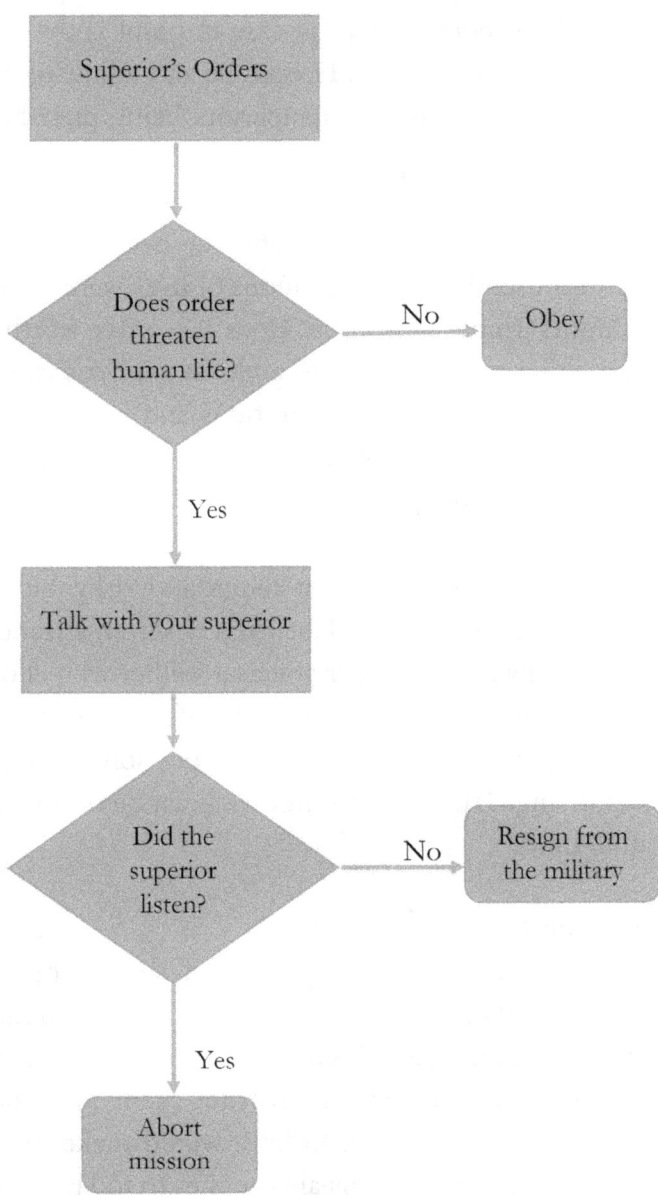

What is even more ironic about obeying these orders is that sometimes, if not most, it is the junior officers that get punished, while the senior officers that gave the order escape without being brought to book. A typical case in point is the story of Henry Wirz of Camp Sumter. He said he was following orders, yet there are no records of his superiors being punished. He faced the music alone.

So dear soldier, would you be able to bear the fact that hundreds, thousands, or even millions of lives were wasted on your account? Think about this. Does the order worth more than human life or the burden of guilt on your conscience? If today's soldier considers these questions and provides honest answers to them, they will be the beacon of light that will guide the soldier through the path of peace.

—Your second option may seem tough and risky, but it is a much better one. You may be labelled a deserter, a traitor, but posterity will always remember you as a soldier who chose the value of life even at the detriment of self. I understand that what I am suggesting is uncomfortable, but sometimes, truth is discomforting. Truth is hard. But we must be on the side of truth at *all* times.

- *Do not frown*
  Have you ever seen a samurai smile? A samurai always wears a serious look; always in a combatant mood. This is understandable, yet Musashi admonished warriors not to frown. While he did not instruct them to smile, the expressions he asked them to have would make their face pleasant to look at. And this also applies to today's soldier.

ON THE SOLDIER'S PATH

Dear soldier, you are a human being to be loved and appreciated, not a person to be feared. Being a soldier shouldn't make you lose touch with your emotions. Be friendly. Be cordial.

It was beautiful to see female army officers participate in "Don't Rush" Challenge on Tik Tok. It showed that military personnel can have fun too. And this is what it should be. The public should not perceive you as someone who is unreachable, someone who doesn't have their interest at heart. Let civilians not be gripped by fear when they see you. They are not your enemies.

- *The body, from the shoulders down to the toes, is one piece*
  These words of Musashi apply to the army as a unit. Soldiers should understand that they are representatives of the military. Anything they do or say off the battlefield would affect, either positively or negatively, how people perceive the military.

The core function of the army is to serve the people, defend the nation, and keep the peace. Your actions or inactions as a soldier should not make the people question this purpose. The military is *one* unit, one *body*. So what you do as an individual soldier tells a lot on the entire unit. You have to position yourself rightly at all times.

Gaze
The second prerequisite for swordsmanship outlined by Musashi is gaze. For Musashi, having vision is not enough, the warrior should also know how to use his vision. He instructed warriors that their vision *must* be wide. And this applies to today's soldier too.

Dear soldier, have a holistic view of situations. Let your vision be wide just like an expanse of blue ocean. Do not be myopic. Do not give in to prejudice. When you have a broad view of a situation, you would be able to make sound decisions that would bring glory to your nation.

In chapter one, we saw the story of Desmond Doss. Doss became a lifetime hero because he had a broad view of the situation at Hacksaw Ridge. While other officers, panicky and hopeless, left the wounded to die, Doss *saw* that the wounded could be saved. While other officers thought that the only way to become a soldier is to wield a rifle, Doss proved to them and the world that lives can also be saved without a rifle.

A soldier needs to understand that many issues of life are multifaceted, thus there is no one-size-fits-all approach to solve these issues. To effectively solve these issues, the soldier must factor in all the nuances present and find out the best possible approach that would not be detrimental to humanity.

Musashi divided gaze or vision into two: Perception and Sight. He wrote: *With perception, you look to feel; with sight, you look see. Perception is strong, sight is weak.* And I agree with Musashi.

A lot of people these days have only sight without perception. Hinging on Musashi's definition, I would give two simple equations:

$$Vision + Emotion = Perception$$
$$Vision - Emotion = Sight$$

ON THE SOLDIER'S PATH

We are emotional beings, and losing touch of our emotions for whatever reason would only reduce us to robotic entities. War crimes are committed by soldiers who only see but don't perceive. Sight is limited, perception is limitless. Soldiers who use the power of the gun to intimidate innocents are myopic. Cold-hearted and emotionless, these soldiers *see* only the present—the quick profit of killing for money, the instant pleasure of rape. They are so insensitive to perceive how their actions would affect their victims, how it would also cause a dent to their image as soldiers.

Dear soldier, your military trainings should toughen your physical body, not harden your heart. Be in touch with your emotions. The world does not revolve around you. Understand that a single action from you is capable of destroying millions of lives. So look at the big picture before acting. Go beyond seeing. Perceive. This is the fundamental step to peace.

Musashi also made another striking point when he wrote: *It is important in strategy that you know your opponent's sword by just looking at it.*

We have likened loyalty to the samurai's sword. So knowing your opponent's sword without looking at it means that you, as a soldier, should be able to detect where the allegiances of the enemy (or even other officers) lie. And the only way to achieve this is through perception. Through perception, you would be able to tell the intentions of the other person through his actions.

An instruction may look good on the surface, but when the soldier goes beyond seeing to perceiving, he would see the flaws and dangers in such an instruction. For instance, one may say that Lieutenant-General Ishii Shiro's objective of making Japan a world power through science was a noble one. Every country aspires to become one of the leading nations of the world, politically, economically, and socially. But a person who doesn't mind using human subjects to carry out deadly experiments does not have the interest of the world at heart.

Sight would tell a Japanese soldier that it is for the good of Japan, but Perception would say that it is not only detrimental to Japan but also to the entire world. Someone may argue that Shiro used human subjects from China and Russia, and so he wouldn't inflict harm on his countrymen. This is a shallow reasoning. A person who does not value life wouldn't hesitate to destroy lives for his selfish gains whether those lives are his countrymen or not. Or didn't Bashar al-Assad of Syria kill fellow Syrians (including children) with sarin gas?

Soldier, perception is a vital quality for you to have. Your ability to perceive the actions of another may be the only step towards saving your country from chaos. Don't be rigid with your ideas. Let your mind be as soft as water, as fluid as a stream unhindered by rocks. Recognize diverse views. Remove the extraneous. Digest them. Then mix them in the melting pot of your heart to produce a single action that would be favorable to all of humanity.

After detailing posture and gaze as prerequisites of swordsmanship, Musashi also taught the warrior how to hold his sword. We are going to look at some of the instructions he gave.

- *A loose grip on a sword is bad*
  In chapter one, we established that a sword, whether the katana or the wakizashi, represents loyalty. So here, we would interpret Musashi's words to mean that your loyalty shouldn't be shaken, no matter what. Hold tenaciously to it. Your loyalty to humanity is paramount above any personal principles or superior orders.

Let your loyalty not be bought with money or with the promise of power. A loose grip on loyalty is bad. When people notice that you do not have a firm hold on loyalty, you lose the trust of the good guys and fall into the exploitative trap of the bad guys.

So make your stand clear—that you are always for humanity. And posterity will reward and remember you forever.

- *When drawing the sword, think of it only as an object to cut down an opponent. As you cut down your opponent, do not change your grip. Hold the sword in such a way that the hand is not weakened.*

Dear soldier, your enemy is not your fellow human being, but the systems that keep stripping peace off the world. And your only goal should be to "cut down" these systems. Yes, in the process you may have to cut down the human beings that promote these systems, but they are not the real enemies.

In cutting down your opponent, hold tenaciously to your sword. Never change your grip. Do not be inconsistent with loyalty. Believe in humanity and be firm with this belief, for this is the only way your "hand would not be weakened."

Desmond Doss never believed in taking human life for whatever (valid) reason, and he held firmly to it. Despite being persecuted, he was resolute, knowing that the rules of the military and the tears of his wife and the pleas of his father do not supersede his belief—his value for life. And this introduces us to Musashi's next lesson: The five approaches for wielding the sword.

The Five Approaches for Wielding the Sword

For me, these five approaches do not only show the warrior where to attack the opponent, but also instructs the warrior on the possible positions where the opponent can launch an attack from. These five approaches are: the first or middle approach, second or up approach, third or down approach, fourth or left approach, and fifth or right approach.

Today's soldier needs to know that the peace he is trying to keep can be threatened through any of these approaches. And to find out how this can happen, we would have to use, again, metaphors.

The middle (first) approach signifies you, the soldier.
The up (second) approach signifies your superiors.
The down (third) approach is the opposing camp.
The left (fourth) approach is your loved ones (family and friends).
The right (fifth) approach signifies your colleagues.
So how can peace be threatened through these different individuals?

You: The Middle Approach

When you enthrone your ideologies or desires above peace, then you are a threat to peace. Although villainous military officers throughout history used their subordinates to carry out their actions, it doesn't take away the fact that these villains did not care about peace or sanctity of life. They were only concerned about their selfish and wicked desires, and because of this, the peace of the world was threatened. There are families who have been scarred for life and races (e.g. the Jews) whose history have never remained the same because of the personal interests of a person or a group of persons.

So dear soldier, understand that sometimes the enemy of peace is not outside, but within. And you can be that enemy. The only way you wouldn't be an enemy is if you always put peace and humanity first. This cannot be emphasized enough.

Superiors: The Up Approach

As we have seen in some stories shared, most of the havoc that have been wreaked on humanity by the military were instigated by senior officers. Think about it: from Adolf Hitler to Saddam Hussein to Idi Amin.

Army officers like the people mentioned above, work their way to the top so that they can have the influence to carry out their nefarious acts. They use the junior officers as pawns to fulfill their desires. Sometimes, they use force and threats to get the junior officers to do their biddings, while at other times, they persuade them through words.

Hitler, for example, was a great orator. He used his oratorical prowess to get Germans to believe that the Jews were a threat to the growth of Germany. As a matter of fact, Hitler wrote in his book, *Mein Kampf*: "I know that men are won over less by the written than by the spoken word, that every great movement on this earth owes it growth to great orators and not to great writers." And through his speeches, he got his countrymen to *hate* the Jews and almost exterminated them.

Dear soldier, threat to peace may come from your superiors. And when this happens, you have to make a decision whether to obey the last order or be on the side of humanity. I have already given you an algorithm.

The Opponent: The Down Approach
We already know that when two or more nations are in a war, they are threatening or tearing down the peace of their nations. This is one way peace can be threatened with the down approach. But another way we often do not take cognizance of is the situation where the opposing nation(s) lure the soldier of the other nation to deliberately sabotage the peace of his nation.

In chapter one, we saw examples of traitors who betrayed their nations to the enemy for fame, power, money, or all three. Soldiers do not just become saboteurs overnight. Saboteurs are individuals who already lack scruples before joining the army. And when the enemy spots them, he uses them to his advantage to carry out his vile plans.

This is the reason you ought to be upright, dear soldier. When you are morally upright, when you understand what is ethical, when you value the sanctity of human life, then you wouldn't be the weak link on the chain that holds peace.

Loved ones: The Left Approach
I used our loved ones to represent the left approach because of this: the heart, which is the center of our emotions, is at the left side of the body. The loved ones of a soldier can cajole him to disrupt the peace of the people.

There are stories of families who go about disturbing others because they feel they are untouchable since they have a family member or friend in the military. Military personnel have been used by their families or friends to intimidate other civilians.

Dear soldier, do not be part of this. Do not allow those you love use you as a tool to disrupt the mental, physical, or emotional wellbeing of others. Let them know that you are in the military to serve, not to bully. Your gun is for restoring peace not for instilling fear. Remember that the soldier has to have an upright posture. Let your loved ones understand this.

Colleagues: The Right Approach
Human beings are social animals, and as behavioral science has shown, we pick many of habits from others. It is for this reason that soldiers can be and are influenced by peer pressure. Soldiers learn harmless traits from their colleagues, like drinking, looking good for the opposite sex, and buying things they don't need. Some people have even joined the military because they have friends in the military.

But just like harmless traits are learned, toxic behavior and vile actions can also be learned. If you read novels or watch movies about war, you would see that there are some soldiers who commit crimes like raping and killing innocents, not because it is in their nature to do so, but because they are cajoled by other officers and they don't want to be left out.

Dear soldier, you have to remember again the need to be upright. Through uprightness, you can distinguish right from wrong. Emulate the good. Eschew the bad. Have a firm, independent mind that cannot be pushed into doing wrong. If influence must come into play, let your colleagues be the ones that would be influenced by your (good) actions.

Now that you have seen the different approaches by which peace can be threatened, there is a salient principle Musashi taught: *Position – No Position.*

The Principle of Position No-Position

This principle is like a contradiction of the five approaches because Musashi wrote:

> *Position – no position means that there is no such thing as sword positions* [or approaches]. *No matter the opponent's approach, the terrain, the circumstances, or sword, always have the intention of cutting down the opponent easily.*

While this looks like a contradiction, it actually is not. All Musashi was trying to say is that the warrior shouldn't be focused only on the possible approaches the opponent might use to attack, because if the warrior focuses on them alone, then there is a tendency for his swordsmanship to become rigid and mechanical. Musashi wanted the warrior to flexible—to be able to move in and out of positions, having just one aim in mind: to cut down the enemy. This is why he wrote:

When in the upper position, you can gently lower your sword and adopt the middle posture. Also, when in the middle posture, you can move up a bit and adopt the upper position. In the lower position, you could move up a bit and take up the middle position. Depending on the condition, if you are on the left or right side and you move towards the center, it basically becomes the middle or lower position.

This applies to the soldier too. Don't focus on one approach, thinking that that's the only way peace can be threatened. For instance, you may think that your superiors or opposing nation are the threats to peace, without knowing that the ones close to you are even bigger threats.

So be flexible to read the situation and block every loophole. You can counter one approach with another. Your colleagues can stand with you against the unethical orders from your superior. You, as the middle approach, can educate your loved ones on what it means to serve the nation. You can report erring officers to your superiors for disciplinary action. You can inform your superiors on the plans of the opposing nation. This is the flexibility Musashi recommended. This is position – no position.

Dear soldier, be like water: flexible, yet forceful. Still, yet stretching. Water is an indispensable resource; a requirement for survival for all living things. In the same way, you are an indispensable requirement for the peace of your nation and the world at large. Water comes in diverse forms and you can take up any form: you can be the rain dousing the tensions of the world, or the flowing stream carrying the debris of intimidation and unrest, or the expansive ocean spreading peace all around your nation and the world.

Key Point from Musashi: *Have the spirit of a warrior: Today I will beat who I was yesterday, tomorrow I will defeat the less skilled, and later I will defeat the one that is more skilled.*

CHAPTER THREE

FIRE

Fierce As Fire

The fiery side of the soldier is what the world mainly knows. There is a time for the soldier to be fierce. And by fierceness, I don't mean being ruthless to fellow human beings, but being ruthless and resolute to your strategy to restore peace. Have aggressive strategies that would burn off the systems of chaos already planted in the world.

In Musashi's days, other schools of swordsmanship focused on maintaining distance as the best strategy. It was a logical strategy since the warrior has to keep his distance to avoid getting hit, as he looks for an opportunity to strike his adversary. However, Musashi thought and taught differently.

Musashi's strategy was to put the opponent in an awkward position to prevent him from striking. Musashi wrote that the warrior could use some elements to his favor (e.g. the environment). Or he could also make the opponent lose focus by manipulating his psychology.

The Fire scroll in *The Five Spheres* outlines 27 different techniques the warrior could use to apply Musashi's strategy. And we are going to see how today's soldier can also use 20 of these techniques to foster peace.

1. The Topography
Examine the nature of your terrain or environment

This is the first technique Musashi taught the warrior. He instructed the warrior to use his environment to his advantage. And he gave three ways the warrior could achieve this:

- *Sun shouldering*: Musashi wrote that the warrior should stand in such a way that the sun is behind him. But if that isn't possible, then he should position himself in a way that the sun is at his right side. Even if it's an indoor fight, the warrior should ensure that the fire is behind him or at his right side. The reason for this is two-pronged: the warrior would be able to see the opponent clearly, while the opponent wouldn't be able to see.

- *Looking down on the opponent*: Another instruction Musashi gave to the warrior was that he should always ensure that he stands on places that are elevated, so he could "look down on" the opponent.

- *Chasing the opponent to awkward places*: Musashi wanted his students to always chase their opponents into unfavorable terrains like thresholds, lintels, doors, verandas, pillars, and so on. As they chase them to these places, they should not also give them the opportunity to look around and adjust.

So what do this mean for a soldier?

The soldier should study the environment of the nation and/or the world. And by environment, I do not mean physical environment alone, I also mean social, economic and political environment. Systems that threaten the peace use these environments, either singly or in combination, to cause instability and division.

For instance, we saw earlier that the Vietnam War arose as a result of conflicting political ideologies. The French Revolution came as a result of socio-economic issues. The people of France revolted and overthrew the monarchy after being hit by famine, excess taxes, and financial crisis.[1]

Therefore, it is important for the soldier to understand these various elements and how they affect the peace he is trying to restore. Sometimes, restoring peace is not only through force and guns; peace can be restored when the issues affecting these environments are addressed.

So the soldier should ask himself some pertinent questions: *Are the people happy with the political or socioeconomic situation of the nation? Who are the actors using the political or socioeconomic conditions of the nation as a tool to disrupt the peace of the nation? How can we outwit these actors?* To outwit these actors, we apply Musashi's techniques.

— First, sun shouldering. We can interpret this as blocking the loopholes that can be seen as opportunities by these actors to inject unrest. As a soldier, you can spread political consciousness among the people. Teach them that politics should be for the people and by the people. Teach them to know their rights and stand for their rights. Teach them that political parties or ideologies do not matter so long as the people aspiring into office are focused on promoting the social, economic, physical, and political wellbeing of the people. When you have a politically conscious people who know their rights, the antagonists of peace wouldn't outsmart them to promote their selfish interests. If key players in the Vietnam War had understood and agreed that the value for humanity trumps their differing political ideologies, then the war wouldn't have happened.

Also, actors could come from the angle of poverty. There are countries of the world where the people in government have intentionally made the economic climate harsh so that they can use the frustrations of people as tools for unrest. An individual who is without money, without food, and without hope would take out his frustrations on another human being. Such a person may not mind killing or maiming another under the directives of someone higher just because they've been promised a certain sum of money.

Dear soldier, try to close the economic inequality gap. Teach the people not to depend on their government to create wealth. Tell them that in this digital age, there is no excuse for not having digital skills. Mark Zuckerberg did not wait for his financial liberation from the U.S. government, neither did Jack Ma rely on the Chinese government. They got their wealth through their innovation, consistency, and hard work. Now ask yourself: *Will Mark or Jack attempt to do anything to disrupt the peace of their nation or the world, knowing that if the peace of the world is affected their businesses will also be affected?*

When you show people the need to put their innovation to work, they wouldn't have time to carry out the wicked, selfish interests of others.

— Second, look down on the opponent. At the Democratic National Convention during the campaigns of the 2016 presidential election in the United States, Michelle Obama said, "When they go low, we go high." This catchphrase is the best interpretation for Musashi's "Look down on the opponent."

As a soldier, you have to be a step higher than the enemy at every point in time. Antagonists of peace are bereft of key values that bind the world together. Values such as kindness, respect, loyalty, love, and so on. These values go together with peace, so tearing down peace also translates to tearing down these values.

When they treat you unfairly and show hatred, revenge with kindness and love. When they disrespect you, show respect. When they show disloyalty to the nation, maintain undivided loyalty both to your nation and humanity. This is not only a principle that should be in religious books, it is a principle that should be applied at all times. The world has known pain because warring parties keep fighting at the same level—a level of dirt, impunity, and utter disregard for the rule of law and human life. No one is attempting to go high, to elevate himself from the opponent.

Dear soldier, never go low. Look down on your enemy at all times. I believe that when you always remember that the real enemy is not the other soldier but failed systems, you will always be on the side of peace—the place where you would want nothing but peace even if it costs you your ideologies and desires.

— Third, chase the opponent to awkward places. This is similar to the second point. When you elevate yourself above your opponent, he immediately becomes disadvantaged as he has to stretch himself to get to you. The awkward places for the enemies of peace are the values they have lost. Fighting them with these values will leave them confused, because they wouldn't understand how you fight hatred with love, disloyalty with commitment, disrespect with respect. It is often said that two wrongs cannot make a right. You cannot fight evil with evil. Only good can overcome evil.

Another way of chasing the antagonists of peace to awkward positions is to use tools they don't understand or cannot grasp easily. For instance, recall that I said that some countries deliberately harshen the economy so that they can exploit the poverty of the people. But in this era, one can beat them to their game. How? Through information technology. Take the fight to the internet. Information technology has given people financial liberation. From Mark Zuckerberg to Jack Ma, Bill Gates to Jeff Bezos, Elon Musk to Larry Page, Jack Dorsey to Jerry Yang, Zhang Yiming to Satoshi Nakamoto.

In the internet is a world as real as our physical world. And the beauty of it is that anyone can be anything on the internet.

A person does not need to go through the bureaucratic hassles associated with government policies before gaining wealth. So dear soldier, advise people to liberate themselves financially by taking advantage of tools that would be "awkward" for their oppressors.

2. The Three Initiatives

Every battle begins with one of three initiatives. Because an initiative can determine the winner from the beginning, taking an initiative is the most important thing in strategy.

Musashi outlined three initiatives to forestall the enemy:

- *Advance Initiative*: This is when the warrior takes the initiative to attack. Musashi instructed the warrior to be quick and strong outwards, but calm inwards. He advised the warrior to make the most of their mental strength.

- *Postponed Initiative*: This is when the enemy takes the initiative to attack. Musashi instructed the warrior to relax and pretend to be weak when the enemy takes the initiative to attack. Then when he attacks, the warrior can now "explode" and reveal his strength. He advised the warrior to find a loophole in the opponent's rhythm and capitalize on it to win.

- *Simultaneous Initiative*: This is when both the warrior and the enemy attack at the same time. In this initiative, the warrior does the opposite of what the enemy does. Musashi instructed the warrior to approach the opponent calmly but strongly if the enemy approaches him quickly. Then when the enemy gets to him, he can "explode" and attack. If the enemy at any time relaxes, Musashi advised the warrior to strike forcefully and take victory on the spot. If, on the other hand, the enemy approaches the warrior calmly, then the warrior should approach him quickly. Musashi made a striking point when he wrote: *When he approaches, you approach him once to test your sword, then adjust your attack according to his condition and cut violently to win.*

So what do these three initiatives mean to today's soldier?
The battle for peace is a continuous one because we live in a world with degenerated systems. This is why the soldier must first study his environment before knowing the initiative to take.

— First, the soldier can use the advance initiative. This means taking the battle to the antagonists of peace. How does he do this? The primary way to do this is by disrupting the systems that have been established to take away peace from the nation or the world. I have mentioned earlier how the soldier can promote political and socioeconomic growth among his people. By doing that, he is launching the attack before the enemy does.

— Second, he can use the postponed initiative. Here, he waits for the antagonists of peace to deal all their cards. He observes them and their actions. This can take months to years. He watches their strategy, how they build their systems. Then when he has gotten all the information he needs, he can now attack.

Now this does not mean that the soldier would fold his arms doing nothing, as he watches the antagonists succeed in taking peace out of the nation—or the world. In a duel, a samurai does not watch and do nothing as he is being attacked; he would definitely defend himself. So in the same way, as the antagonists attack first, the soldier must defend and/or attack till he wins.

— Third, he can use the simultaneous initiative. And this is the initiative I prefer for the soldier. Personally, I think a lot has gone wrong with the world for the soldier to waste any more time. Therefore, he has attack just as the enemy is attacking too. The antagonists of peace are *continuously* planning on ways to disrupt law and order for their benefit, and unfortunately they have the economic and political power to do so. This means that the soldier has to be smart in order to outwit them. When they attack strongly, relax so they cannot predict your next move. When they relax thinking you cannot do anything, then you attack. And always remember to adjust your move according to their condition. If the simultaneous initiative is to be summed up in two words, it is this: *be unpredictable*.

3. Pressing Down A Pillow
Don't allow the opponent lift his head

A samurai should not allow his opponent lift his head during combat. Musashi noted that it is bad for the warrior to let his opponent move him around and place him on the defensive. It should be the other way round. Musashi also advised the warrior not to get distracted because the opponent would also have the same intention of attack. Musashi wrote: *In strategy, you must stop the opponent before he attacks, strike the opponent before he hits, and pull the opponent out of his strategy before he can strike you back.* When the warrior understands the Way of pressing down the pillow, then he will be able to predict the next move of the opponent—and stop it.

Musashi knew that the opponent may likely want to use the same technique against the warrior, so he instructed the warrior to allow the opponent to do the useless things and not allow him do anything useful. This is an important element in strategy.

Although pressing down the pillow is a useful technique for the warrior, Musashi noted that using the technique continually puts the warrior on the defensive.

How does this apply to the soldier?
The soldier should be able to predict the moves of the antagonists of peace. In today's world it is even easy to predict what the antagonists would do. Throughout history, we have seen the same systems of oppression, division, impunity, and disregard for human life play out across different countries. So there is nothing new.

Today's soldier already knows the angle the antagonists can attack from. As we saw earlier, they can either attack from political sentiments, social issues, or economic climate. Knowing this, the soldier can help forestall this attack by nipping these issues in the bud. And I have already stated ways in which this can be done.

But just like Musashi noted, pressing down the pillow continually puts you on the defensive. It is said that attack is best form of defense. This means that when you keep defending you are (indirectly) attacking—and showing the enemy all your moves. In plain words, you are giving them the upper hand. So do not use the technique of pressing down the pillow as your only strategy.

4. Crossing the Ford

> *When you are striving towards a goal, have the same determination like you are "crossing the ford"*

To explain this technique, Musashi likened the warrior to a sailor. Crossing the ford means setting sail even when the sailor's friends choose to remain in the harbor. It means knowing the route, knowing the integrity of the ship, and knowing the wind. When the sailor has understood all these, he can now set sail. And if the wind changes few miles to his destination, he must cover the remaining distance with his oars.

It is the same for the warrior: he must understand his strong points and discern the enemy's capability, then "cross the ford" at an advantageous point. Musashi defined crossing the ford as attacking the enemy's weak point and gaining the advantage.

What does this mean for a soldier?
The most important lesson I want the soldier to get from this is this: *When you are striving towards a goal, have the same determination like you are "crossing the ford."* Determination is the operative word. The fight to restore is peace is a tough one. The enemy is not relenting. And there are times when you'd feel like giving up because you think your efforts are fruitless. But that is not true.

Before setting out on this journey to restore peace, you've already counted the cost. You knew that the orchestrators of chaos are ruthless in their dealings. So never be deterred. Fight their ruthlessness with your fierceness.

Try to get your colleagues or friends or family along in this fight, but if they choose to remain at the harbor, let them be. Don't allow them discourage you. For love of country, for love of humanity—this should be your motto. As long as you don't get discouraged, the enemy will definitely get weakened, then you can take your victory.

5. Understanding the Situation

Perceive the enemy's weakness and strength

Musashi wrote that before going to a battle, it is important to understand the intentions of the enemy including his terrain and dispositions. The warrior should also understand the adjustments to the enemy's rhythm and know how to seize the advantage. Then he should use all the information gathered to his advantage to counter all the actions of the enemy. To be able do this effectively, you should have a high intellectual capacity.

Throughout this book, I have emphasized the need for studying all the moves of the enemy. I have also given methods on how this can be done. But in this technique, Musashi made an important point. He stated that the warrior needs to have a high intellectual capacity to be able to understand the situation. And I agree.

Dear soldier, stretch your intellectual capacity through reading. In books lie vital clues for liberation and peace. The antagonists of peace across the world have used similar strategies to carry out their plans. Fortunately, these strategies have been documented in numerous books. And to win the battle, you must read. It is interesting to note that these antagonists know the power of and in books, and they go ahead to try and stop people from reading. For instance, there are countries where history has been scrapped from their academic curriculum. Another example that easily comes to mind is the Nazi book burning of 1933. An event German poet, Henrich Heine saw coming more than hundred years earlier when he wrote in 1821: "Where books are burned, in the end people will be burned."

From May 10, 1933, Nazi-dominated student groups started the public burning of books they tagged "un-German." These books included works from Jewish, liberal, and leftist writers. Over 25,000 volumes were destroyed in the bonfire. Targeted authors included socialists like Bertolt Brecht and August Babel; founder of the concept of communism, Karl Marx; critics like Arthur Schnitzler, an Austrian playwright; and authors they called "corrupting foreign influences" like Ernest Hemingway.[2]

The antagonists of peace know the power in the written word. In a short film by the United States Holocaust Memorial Museum[3], Azar Nafisi, the author of *Reading Lolita in Tehran* said: "Books represent humanity at its best and its worst. [And] The first thing every totalitarian regime does along with confiscation and mutilation of reality, is confiscation of history and confiscation of culture. I think they both happen almost simultaneously."

Ruth Franklin, a literary critic and contributing editor in *The New Republic*, gave a reason why totalitarian regimes do this. She said: "All literature is dangerous to a regime that fears the free flow of ideas because the literature, in its most fundamental way, is meant to forge connections among human beings." And this fear is triggered by the unpredictability of literature, just like author Nafisi rightly noted. ". . . You don't know where it takes you. Knowledge is always unpredictable; there is always a risk. It is like Alice jumping down that hole, running after that white rabbit, not knowing where she goes. And for tyrants, control is the main thing. They don't like this unpredictability, they don't want the citizens to connect to the unknown parts of themselves, of their past, and to connect to the world," she said.

Corroborating Nafisi's words, Franklin added that, ". . . these [totalitarian] regimes are predicated on the idea that the people within them will resign themselves to thinking that this is all there is. And that there aren't any other options."

So dear soldier, you have to defeat the aim of the antagonists of peace. There are other options. War, murders, and the gross undervaluation of human life aren't the only way. There are a lot of options "hidden" within books. In books, you will learn the operations of these antagonists. You will see the world in all its entirety. You will see and piece together the puzzle of humanity. In books, you will see what is meant to be, and what ought not to be.

6. The Collapse

Everything has the tendency to collapse

Musashi wrote: "Everything has the tendency to collapse. A house can collapse, a body can collapse, and an enemy can collapse when the time comes and their rhythm becomes chaotic."

He went further to instruct the warrior to be observant and notice when the enemy falters and begins to collapse. This is the point the warrior can claim victory. If the warrior allows the moment to slip away, the enemy may recover and become defensive thereafter.

In this moment of collapse, Musashi advised the warrior to be direct and vigorous with his attack. "Smash the enemy to pieces so that he cannot recover," he wrote.

What does this mean for the soldier?
Musashi noted that everything has a tendency to collapse. And this is true. However, I will like to add that there are three things that can cause an entity to collapse.

- *Faulty foundation*: A house with a faulty foundation would definitely collapse. A person with a congenital heart condition would collapse.
- *Age*: An old house would likely collapse. People also collapse when they become old.
- *Pressure*: An excavator or a storm can collapse a house. A person can also collapse if they are hit.

Now when it comes to fighting the antagonists the peace, you must understand that their ideologies aren't built on a faulty foundation. This is why it has lasted for decades. So the soldier cannot hope that these ideologies would collapse because of a faulty foundation. That is impossible.

We cannot also rely on age. The solidity of these ideologies and the consequent indoctrination that follows have made these ideologies to persist for a long time. Thus, the soldier cannot also hope that these ideologies would wane as time goes by.

The only thing left for the soldier is pressure. Attack. The antagonists may be rigid and resolute to their ideologies and actions, but as you attack, as you keep up with the pressure, a time will come when they will falter and begin to collapse. Be observant to recognize this moment and ensure you take victory at this point. Musashi called it "smashing into debris"— breaking the enemy to a point where recovery is impossible.

7. Becoming the Enemy

The one trapped in the house is a pheasant and the one who comes in to cut him down is a hawk

This technique is simple, but Musashi adds to it a layer of depth. He said bandits are often considered powerful when they are trapped in a house during a robbery. But if one puts oneself in the position of a bandit, then one would discover that the bandit is actually weak. Trapped in a house, the bandit feels that the world is against them; he feels desperate and hopeless. At that point he is a pheasant and the one after him, a hawk.

Musashi noted that when the warrior feels that the enemy is strong, he would always find it difficult to attack. But when the warrior thinks of himself as the enemy, he would be able to predict the mental and emotional dispositions of the enemy, and discover the most effective point to hit him.

What does this mean for the soldier?
Dear soldier, do what the antagonists failed to do. The world is in this state today because the enemies of peace have never tried to see themselves as the people they were suppressing. They have never asked themselves how their actions or inactions would affect their nation or the world. They have zero empathy. And that is why the world is a torn fabric of chaos.

Soldier, you have to see yourself as the enemy, not to act like them, but to know their weak points. When you put yourself in the position of the enemy, you would realize that they aren't as strong as you feared. You would be able to know their next move, possible mistakes, thought patterns, and expectations. With these information, you can then formulate an effective plan for attack.

8. Releasing Four Hands

If you think there is going to be a deadlock, give up your intention immediately and use some other advantageous tactics to win

A situation may arise during a duel or a battle where both the warrior and his opponent have the same intentions and when this happens, the fight becomes a deadlock. This is the spirit of "four hands." In such a situation, Musashi instructed the warrior to give up the intention and try another advantageous tactic. The warrior should not advance at this point, rather he should re-strategize and achieve victory using tactics that the enemy cannot think of.

Dear soldier, in this fight to restore peace, there are times when it would look like you have dealt all your cards yet you are not winning, and the enemy is not winning too. Don't keep trying out the same things over and over again, expecting a different result. Break the deadlock. Analyze the situation and then come back with a better strategy. Don't get attached to one strategy. Be flexible enough to move in and out of strategies depending on the prevailing circumstances. This is the only way you can be ahead of the enemy.

9. Moving the Shade

Reveal the enemy's intentions and you will instantly realize where your advantage lies

There are situations where the warrior wouldn't know the true intentions of the enemy because his sword is either by his side or behind him. This is because the enemy "shades" his intentions. To uncover the intentions of the enemy, Musashi recommended that the warrior "moves the shade." What this means is that the warrior should act as if he wants to launch an attack. This will ruffle the enemy and then his true intentions would be known. When the warrior moves the shade, he not only uncovers the enemy's intention, but also realizes the advantage he, the warrior, has. At this point, the warrior should never let his guard down, else the opportunity would slip away.

ON THE SOLDIER'S PATH

How does this apply to a soldier?

I have observed that the antagonists of peace are smart. They seldom reveal their true intentions so that they can make the people believe that they have nothing to worry about. In the short film by the United States Holocaust Memorial Museum, Robert Behr, one of the survivors of the concentration camp, said that there were warning signs, but people like his mother never took them seriously. He said he remembers asking his mother if they should be worried about Hitler but she said to him, "No. We are living in a democracy. We have the protection of the police. Nobody's going to hurt us." But in the end they were arrested and sent to a concentration camp.[4]

In times when you cannot accurately tell what the plans of the enemy are, feint an attack. If the antagonists of peace have bad intentions, they would retaliate, even in a more brutal manner. But if they have good intentions, they would most likely ask why the attack happened and assure you that they mean no harm.

For a soldier, skepticism is a gift, so you may also think that their call for dialog and explanation is a ploy to get you to relax before they strike. True, that is possible. However, you have to remember that the antagonists do not value life. Surprising them with an attack would definitely ruffle them and they would have no choice but to show what they were planning all along. They would have no time to think about any more strategy. They would also think that one way or another you may have been privy to their plans, so they'd need to launch an attack before it is too late. This moment of unsettlement and destabilization is the right time to launch your real attack and finish them off.

10. The Contagious

To weaken your opponent, infect him…

Musashi wrote that many things are contagious. Drowsiness is contagious, yawning is contagious, even time is contagious. The warrior can get his enemy to a disadvantaged position by transferring his own disposition to him.

For instance, if the warrior notices that the enemy is agitated, the warrior can remain calm, and when the enemy sees this calmness, he would also relax and his will to attack would be dampened. This is the point where the warrior strikes. As a final admonition, Musashi wrote: *To weaken your opponent, infect him with a melancholic feeling, then hopelessness, and lastly weakness.*

So how does a soldier infect the enemies of peace?
The soldier can do this in two ways. It is either he infects the enemy with the true ideology that should govern living, or he infects them with a false strategy.

The first can be done through dialog. The soldier can educate these antagonists on the need for peace. He would teach them the workings of peace and how it is beneficial to all. However, I must admit that infecting the antagonists of peace with this ideology is nearly impossible. They know what peace is, but since they want to profit from chaos, they would rather hinder peace from thriving.

In 2020, there have been demonstrations across continents of the world—from Europe to Asia to Africa. These demonstrations arise because of maladministration and also the deliberate attempt to undermine the value of human life and, consequently, stifle human rights. For example, in Philippines, the anti-terrorism bill was signed into law by the president. Hearing "anti-terrorism," one would think that the law is actually harmless and geared towards protecting Filipinos, but that is not the case. The law stifles the rights of the average Filipino. A part of the law states that suspects could be jailed without charge for weeks. It also classifies terrorism as "engaging in acts intended to endanger a person's life," intended to "damage public property" or "interfere with critical infrastructure," where the purpose is to intimidate the government. With this law, citizens no longer have the right to protest against bad governance. However, the law states that it does not intend to punish advocacy, protest, dissent, industrial action and strikes, so long as they don't create "a serious risk to public safety."[5] But only the government can define what constitutes a risk to public safety and what does not.

Now a government that passes such a law does not have the interest of the people at heart. It is a law that can be taken advantage of to harm even those that promulgated it. It has been noted that the government that signed this law has a "poor human rights record,"[6] so how can such a government understand the language of the peace. Because of situations like this, the best thing to do is to infect the antagonists with a false strategy.

When you know that the enemies of peace are on their toes, draw back and relax. Make them feel like they have succeeded in scaring you away. Make them relax. Make them consider you as weak and insignificant. Make them underestimate you. When they have done this, then you hit them with everything you have got. Their greatest weapon is oppressing and suppressing the people. However, if you can get the people to rise and speak up for themselves, then you would leave the enemies of peace confused. And therein lies Musashi's next technique.

11. The Confused Opponent

There is confusion in everything

According to Musashi, there are three situations where the enemy can become confused: (1) when he senses danger, (2) when he senses failure, and (3) when he is surprised. Musashi advised the warrior to put his opponent in a state of mental turmoil and should not allow him recover from it. He told the warrior to attack when the enemy least expects without giving him time to think or strategize. As the enemy thinks of his next move, the warrior should take advantage of the situation and win.

Dear soldier, spring the element of surprise on the enemies of peace. Let them see that they are failing. Let them also see the danger in their failure. This would get them confused. With confusion comes panic. And when they panic, you can capitalize on their mistakes to gain victory.

12. To Frighten

People are frightened by the things that they never expected to happen

For Musashi, fright is commonplace and the utmost aim of the warrior is to frighten is opponent. The warrior can frighten the opponent with his *body*, *sword*, or *voice*. When the opponent becomes frightened, the warrior can take advantage of the fear and instability.

How does this apply to today's soldier?
Through observation, I have discovered that the enemies of peace keep eroding systems that promote peace because they think the people weak. But when the people would finally arise, the enemies of peace would become frightened. Therefore, just as Musashi said, aim to frighten your enemy.

You can *frighten them with your sword*. In this book we have explained that the sword is a metaphor for loyalty. The enemies of peace are often stereotypical, so they may think that they could easily buy your allegiance. But *never* let this happen. Let them know that your allegiance is on the side of truth, and because of that you are going to employ the two other ways to make them afraid.

Frighten them with your body. Remember earlier, I advised you to liberate the minds of people by educating them on the tenets of peace and why they should demand peace. When you have done that, you would have a large body of people who would never rest until the atmosphere for peace has been created or restored. With this body of people, the last method of making the enemy afraid can now be employed.

Frighten them with your voice. Do not lose your voice for whatever reason. Let your voice be loud. Let it resonate to the ends of the earth. The enemies of peace are always against those who speak the truth. This is why military dictators arrest or even murder journalists, writers, activists, and everyone who is bold enough to speak. But that should not discourage you. As long as your voice remains loud, the enemy would become frightened. Your voice should be heard on the streets, on social media, in newspapers, in media houses. Every platform you have, gives you the opportunity to speak out. Because a loud voice can attract allies, never allow the enemy mute your voice.

13. Soaking in

If you separate yourself from the opponent, you will not win

This is like a situation of "four hands," but instead of withdrawing and re-strategizing, Musashi told the warrior to "soak in" or merge with the enemy. Unlike other techniques where Musashi gave the warrior definite ways to take advantage and win, here, he told the warrior to understand the situation and figure out how to take victory through it.

So what does this mean for the soldier in his fight for peace? There are times when the soldier would have to blend in. You would have to do this not because you've been bought over, but because you actually want to know the plans of the enemy. In these times, you would be a Trojan horse. Soak into the enemy. Absorb into their systems. Know how they work. See their strengths and weaknesses. Then use this information to strategize how to create an atmosphere for peace.

14. The Hurting Corners

It is difficult to move strong things by pushing directly, so you have to "hurt the corners"

Here, Musashi recommended that the enemy should be weakened from "the corners." According to him, if the corners are overthrown, the whole body will also be overthrown.

Today's soldier can also apply the same technique. Sometimes, you don't win by hitting directly. You have to be patient to get your ultimate goal. Weakening the corners is like gaining small victories. For instance, your ultimate goal is to achieve peace. However, knowing that the enemy wouldn't grant this easily, you can weaken the corners by establishing other needs like respect for human rights, sound education, and so on. Individually, these are not the ultimate goal, but collectively, they sum up to it. If the enemy starts to respect human rights, it would give people the confidence to demand for changes in the society that affect their peace. In the same vein, a sound education broadens the mind of people to know how they have been exploited, and since knowledge is the first step to freedom, these people would also start clamoring for a change.

So dear soldier, when you cannot hit the enemy directly, chip away the corners of his structure until all of it crumbles.

15. The Three Shouts

Voice is a quality of life

Musashi stated that there are three times a warrior can shout in a fight: *before*, *during*, and *after*. Before the fight, the warrior shouts as loudly as he can. During the fight, his voice is low-pitched. After the fight, he gives a shout of victory. Shouting is important because voice is a quality of life. It shows strength.

In the 12th technique, "To frighten," I have already stated the importance of not being silent as the soldier fights for peace. However, I will like to add a salient point: Many shout when they are not supposed to. The shout of victory should be reserved till the end of the fight. So what this means in essence dear warrior, is that do not celebrate early. Ensure you have totally defeated the enemy before giving a shout of victory. Giving a shout when the battle is not over may cause your allies to withdraw because they think the battle is over. Do not give a shout a victory when the fight has not even started. Claim your victory, then shout.

16. The Mountain-Sea Transformation

It is bad to repeat an action in the midst of a battle with an enemy

This technique can be summed up into Albert Einstein's words: "The definition of insanity is doing the same thing over and over again and expecting a different result." Musashi told the warrior never to repeat the same move during a battle. Although, there are times when the warrior can repeat a move twice, Musashi noted that it is totally bad to repeat it the third time.

When the warrior launches an attack on the enemy and it fails, then he should try out a different approach. Musashi summarized this technique thus: *When the opponent thinks of* the "mountain" then you attack with "sea." But if he thinks of the "sea" then you attack with the "mountain."

Dear soldier, be strategic in your actions. Don't keep doing the same things that do not work. The absence of peace we experience now in different continents of the world have persisted for centuries. If the world still experiences it, it means that those who had attempted to solve this situation were doing the same things that have never worked.

I think in restoring peace, many have only focused on cutting off the rotting branches instead of uprooting the entire tree. As long as the root is still buried beneath the earth, new branches would still be corrupted. Just as I mentioned in chapter one, the absence of peace is simply a product of the total disregard for the sanctity and value of life. This is the root of the problem. So all your actions, dear soldier, should be geared towards solving this problem. And this leads to the next technique of Musashi.

17. Pulling the Bottom Out

> *You have to silence the enemy's spirit by pulling his heart out from below...*

All Musashi was saying here is: deal with the root. He advised the warrior to ensure that the enemy is not only defeated at the surface but that his spirit is also defeated, because if the enemy is defeated only at the surface, he may recover. The warrior has to silence the spirit of the enemy for only then can the enemy be *completely* defeated.

I have already discussed dealing with the problem from the root. The antagonists of peace keep transferring their ideology from generation to generation. So to ensure that this issue does not keep sprouting up from generation to generation, it has to be defeated from the roots. The minds of many need reorientation. People need to be given new perspectives. And dear soldier, this is your duty.

18. To Renew

When there is no resolution, change your perspective

This tactic is similar to "releasing four hands." It is used when the fight between the warrior and his opponent is unresolved. Musashi advised the warrior to step back, think about the situation in a different perspective, then win with a fresh rhythm. *Without changing the circumstance,* the warrior should change his spirit and win through a different technique.

The difference between "renew" and "releasing four hands" is that while the latter requires that the warrior changes his strategy immediately, the former requires that the warrior steps back a bit and think of a new move.

As a soldier, stick to your cause at all times. But when it looks like there is no resolution in sight, step back a bit, look at the situation from a fresh perspective, then launch a new attack. Check what you are doing wrong. Then readjust. The sole aim is to win, so withdrawing for a while to plan and renew your strength is necessary.

19. The Rat Head – Ox Neck

Whenever you become preoccupied with small details, remember that the Way of the Warrior is always a "rat head - ox neck, rat head - ox neck"

This technique is used when the warrior and the opponent focus on minor details and become confused. Musashi noted that when this happens, the warrior should focus on the important details.

Dear soldier, never be distracted. In the fight for peace, there would be issues planted by the enemy to take your attention off the fight. But be smart to understand this. Always redirect your focus to the important matters. Never allow yourself to be distracted.

20. The Body of a Rock

You have the body of a rock when you attain the Way of the Warrior

This is a culmination of all the techniques above. Musashi wrote that when the warrior masters the Way of Strategy, his body becomes like a rock—nothing can touch him, he cannot be moved.

Dear soldier, be steadfast. Be resilient. Never give up this fight. Use all the tactics mentioned above to transform yourself into a rock. The enemies of peace shouldn't win. And this can only happen if you never give up.

Dear soldier, you are a rock, you are light. Be fierce as fire.

Key Point from Musashi: *The true Way in terms of swordsmanship means fighting with the opponent and winning. This is not replaceable.*

CHAPTER FOUR

WIND

Enigmatic as the Wind

As the wind blows, it sweeps everything that is not firm away. Sometimes, it has the power to uproot firm things like trees, pillars, and houses. The wind is that powerful. It is also enigmatic because one cannot tell where it is coming from or where it is going to. All we know is that it just blows and moves and signifies the advent of something refreshing: rain.

In Musashi's Wind scroll, he criticized the ways of other schools of swordsmanship. Like the wind, his own Way swept away the doctrines of other schools because they had no solid foundation and did not lead to victory. Musashi's Way did lead to victory. After all, he was undefeated in all his duels, including those he fought with samurais from other schools.

To introduce his Way to the warrior, he needed to first puncture holes in the ways of other schools, not because he just wanted to be a critic, but because he knew that there were flaws in those ways.

This is the same thing you should do as a soldier. Before now, there have been individuals and groups who have sought peace, yet failed because they didn't do it the right way. Therefore, it is not enough for me to present a new way to the soldier without also showing why other paths to peace did not or will not work.

The soldier on *this* path of peace is an enigma. His path is different. It is not a path other have treaded. And in this chapter, based on Musashi's ideas, I am going to show the soldier how this path differs from the previous paths to peace.

1. The Extra-Long Swords of Other Sects

Depending on the length of a sword for victory shows a weakness of spirit

Musashi talked about schools of swordsmanship that had a predilection for extra-long swords. He considered them weak schools who depended on the length of their sword to defeat the enemy from a distance. According to him, their mantra was, "More than an inch gives an advantage." But for Musashi, this mantra showed that they did not understand strategy and were unable to grasp its principles.

So what does an extra-long sword mean when it comes to seeking peace?

Recall that we defined a sword as loyalty. This means that when we talk about an extra-long sword, we are talking about being loyal to other people or groups besides your nation or humanity. There are people who believe that they cannot restore peace if they do not show loyalty or fraternize with certain sacred cows. These people feel that they do not have the resources to fight for peace, thus they need extra hands. They want to pass the bulk of the fight to others while they watch from a distance, waiting to take the glory.

There is nothing wrong in seeking allies as you fight for peace, but make sure your allies are those who are also loyal to the nation or humanity. Make sure they are people who want the same thing you want. Because if they are not *truly* on your side, then they would foil your plans to attain peace.

This is why Musashi raised an important point when he said: *If the enemy is close, like so close that you can grapple him, a long sword would make it difficult for you to cut him. The sword becomes useless. You are restricted by the sword and even worse than a person with a short sword or someone without a weapon.*

Musashi's words mean that if there is a situation where you are close to defeating the enemy, it is possible that the extra allies you have would draw you back if they have an interest different from yours. Your loyalty shouldn't be scattered in different places at the same time. Those you are loyal may have interests far different from yours, and may only feign support for you for a short time.

Your loyalty is to your nation and to humanity. And that is enough. Being loyal to your nation and humanity should drive all your actions and guide your strategy. Don't ever think that you cannot win alone or with a small group of people who share your ideologies. Even Musashi asked: *Without carrying a* [extra] *long sword, would someone with a short sword lose*? Not at all. It is a matter of strategy, not the sword.

Musashi also noted that an extra-long sword is useless to someone who is physically weak. So if you don't have the mental, emotional and maybe, physical strength to fight for peace, having extra allies won't help you. The duty lies squarely on your shoulder. Don't pass the job to others.

2. The Strong Long Swords of Other Sects

Trying to swing a sword strongly is a bad thing, and it is difficult to win with such a rough technique

Musashi stated that in swordsmanship, there should be no such thing as a "strong sword" or a "weak sword." Swinging a sword forcefully is bad, and when the warrior tries to cut the enemy too hard because he feels he has a "strong sword" then he would likely fail. Musashi also noted that it is wrong to cut forcefully when the warrior is testing his sword.

All the warrior should think about is cutting down the enemy. He shouldn't cut too strongly, neither should he cut too weakly. He should apply only the right force to defeat the opponent. If the warrior strikes too hard, there is a tendency he may shatter his own sword.

So what does this mean on the soldier's path to peace?
What Musashi was saying was that just like the warrior shouldn't depend on the length of his sword for victory, he shouldn't also depend on the strength of his sword. For the

soldier, this means that he should not be too overconfident. There are those who had rubbished their efforts in bringing peace because they felt they were so strong. They became hotheaded and unwilling to listen and reason. They felt that their loyalty to the cause superseded that of every other person. At a point, they became unable to separate their personal desires and egos from the fight for peace. And because of this, they never even realized the moments when they should have taken victory.

The soldier shouldn't also consider his loyalty to be weak. If he does this, he automatically loses the fight. Any challenge from the enemy can get him to run away from the fight.

So dear soldier, your victory does not and should not depend on how strong you feel you are. Your ego should not be placed before your fight for peace. The strength of your loyalty does not lie on how rigid you are to what you believe in, but in how discerning you are to recognize what action(s) would foster peace. We have already seen in the Water scroll the importance of being flexible. So let your mind be always on the goal.

3. The Short Sword of Other Sects

> *The thought of winning using a short sword is not the true Way. Long and short swords have been clearly explained in ancient times. But they do not matter, all that matters is taking advantage of the situation*

Just like some schools depend on long swords for victory, Musashi noted that there were other schools that depended on a short sword. Samurais of these schools used the short sword with the aim of jumping in and catching the enemy off guard. However, Musashi stated that aiming for the enemy's unguarded moment is a defensive strategy that cannot be used when the enemy is close or when the warrior is surrounded by many rivals.

There are people who have fought for peace and thought they could handle the fight alone. They sprang up from nowhere trying to catch the enemies of peace off guard. And that is a poor strategy, because these enemies have all the resources to stifle the voice of an opposition.

This is why the soldier must strike a balance. On this path of peace, you don't journey alone, yet you do not journey with everyone. Allies are needed. But ensure that your allies are loyal *solely* to the cause. This is the only way to victory.

4. The Sword Techniques of Other Sects

> *When it comes to cutting down a person, there is no special way to do that*

Musashi had a problem with other sects that invented a lot of techniques and taught them to their students without first teaching the students the true Way of the warrior. By doing this, they turned swordsmanship into a commodity for sale. The students went about feeling they knew all there was to swordsmanship, while in truth, they knew nothing.

For Musashi, victory goes beyond techniques. He noted that there is no special way to cut the opponent down. *Whether someone is knowledgeable or ignorant, whether it is a woman or*

ON THE SOLDIER'S PATH

a child attacking, all it takes is stabbing or cutting... The way to win is to cut first, and not pay attention to small details.

Just like in Musashi's time, there are people who have developed their own techniques for attaining peace. They transfer these ideologies to people who don't understand what the fight for peace is all about. They just champion a cause because they see others doing so. At other times, they join the movement because of what they think they would benefit. They fail to understand that the fight is to uproot every element that is limiting the peace of the nation or the world.

A perfect example of this is seen in Colum McCann's novel, *Apeirogon*. The book, mostly based on true accounts, explores the conflict in the Middle East between Palestine and Israel as it relates to two fathers: Bassam Aramin; a Palestinian, and Rami Elhanan; an Israeli. Aramin lost his daughter, Abir when she was shot in the head by an Israeli soldier in 2007; while Elhanan lost his daughter, Smadar in 1997 in a suicide bombing attack carried out by Palestinians.

United by a common pain, these men have been touring the world to propagate peace. They have been in many interviews and delivered a lot of speeches and have passed same message all the time: peace. But there is a place where the story of these men relates to what Musashi said about the techniques of other schools.

Elhanan said that many of his countrymen turned against him because he refused to follow their path of retaliation. He said: "I have been called many things, an insect, an Arab lover, a self-hating Jew. They say I am naïve, self-righteous..."[1] Despite this, he remained resolute to what was right. He knew that revenge wouldn't bring the peace Israel needed, the peace he needed. He just wanted the path that led to peace and that's why he said: "If I had found another path I would have taken it—I don't know, revenge, cynicism, hatred, murder. But I am a Jew. I have great love for my culture and my people and I know that ruling and oppressing and occupying is not Jewish. Being Jewish means that you respect justice and fairness."[2]

Elhanan's words are in line with the principles outlined in this book. The path of peace remains the same, no matter the circumstances. The enemy is not the other human being, but the systems of injustice that have been solidly rooted in the world.

In Musashi's strategy, all it takes for the warrior to win is to make his posture and spirit straight, and also make his opponent weak and fall. In the same way, the soldier should be upright in every way. He should weaken all the actions of the enemy with the deeds of justice, fairness, equality, and value for human life.

5. The Special Sword Positions of Other Sects

The only time to use the "defensive" position is when there is really no opponent

Musashi noted that other schools taught special positions to their students. The positions taught were mainly defensive positions, and Musashi didn't feel it was right. According to him, these positions were drawn from long standing customs and codified into rules, so they had no place in a one-on-one combat. In addition, a defensive stance meant trying to use immobility to one's advantage, and that's not a good trait of a warrior.

The warrior should always take the initiative—he should be proactive. A defensive stance means that the warrior is waiting for others to take the initiative, but this shouldn't be. This was why UAR lost to Israel in 1967, and Western Europe lost to Germany in 1940 just as we saw in chapter one. The UAR and Western Europe allowed the enemy to take the initiative. They were waiting for an attack; they were on the defensive. And by being on the defensive, they gave the enemy the power to control the narrative, to put the odds in their favor. This was the reason Hitler could postpone the attack on Western Europe 29 times in six months. And it is surprising to think that in all those times, Western Europe never thought about launching an attack. They just relaxed, waiting, and dismissing every warning as a false alarm. That is not the true Way of the warrior. A warrior is not careless. A warrior is attentive to details. A warrior understands timing. This is why Musashi told the warrior to: *Do things that the enemy cannot imagine—confuse the enemy, disturb the enemy, or threaten the enemy in order to catch him when his rhythm wavers.*

There are people who claim they want peace, yet they do not take the initiative. They would rather sit still and watch others do the job, then come out to claim the glory. In *Apeirogon*, Rami Elhanan talked about this. He said: "Some people have an interest in keeping the silence. Others have an interest in sowing hatred based on fear. Fear makes money, and it makes laws, and it takes land, and it builds settlements, and fear likes to keep everyone silent . . . We use the word security to silence others. But it's not about that, it's about occupying someone else's life, someone else's land, someone else's head. It's about control. Which is power."[3]

For some people, the path to peace is the path of silence. It is the path of enduring injustice and inequality. It is the path of fear. And fear sets one on edge, it makes one defensive. It makes one skeptical about demanding for the creation of an enabling atmosphere for peace.

But this is not the true way. Dear soldier, you are the wind. They shouldn't see you coming. You are unpredictable. Fear is an emotion that can be predicted. But courage is an element of surprise. Never cower. You know the true path to peace—follow it.

6. Gazing in Other Sects

Once you have trained and grasped the Way of the Warrior, you will also be able to see the distance and speed of any sword.

Musashi observed that other sects teach their students to focus on different things during combat. Some tell their students to focus on the opponent's sword, other teach their students to focus on the opponent's arm or face or feet. Focusing on different things during combat can cause distraction, and Musashi called it "blindness" in strategy.

The warrior should focus on the goal. Musashi exemplified this with a soccer player. A soccer does not have to look at the ball closely before he can perform skills with it. So what is the goal for the warrior? The opponent's mind.

Musashi advised the warrior to not just see, but perceive the opponent's mind. By doing this, he is able to see the strength and weakness of the adversary.

Dear soldier, as you journey towards peace, do not be like others that can be easily distracted. Don't concentrate on the enemy's actions alone; they can be deceptive. The actions of the enemy are minute details; their plans are hidden in their minds. So concentrate on reading the enemy's mind, that way you can predict their next move. Always remember this: If the people of Troy had concentrated on reading the minds of the Greeks, they wouldn't have been carried away by the "gift" of the Trojan horse.

7. Use of the Feet in Other Sects
In our strategy, nothing changes about the footstep

Other schools of swordsmanship during Musashi's day taught their students footwork during combat. Some of the footwork they taught include: floating feet, flying feet, shrugging feet, and so on. According to Musashi, the flying feet made the warrior gallop; the flying feet made him jump and fly; while the shrugging feet made him indecisive.

What Musashi recommended was a firm step. In the Way of Strategy, there is no change to the footstep. The warrior should maintain the same step he uses during his normal walk. He advised the warrior to move according to the rhythm of the opponent. He also should not move too fast so he wouldn't falter, or too slowly because walking slowly may make him miss the opportunity to take victory.

Some people have failed to achieve peace because they were either in a haste or they were indecisive. Hasty—because they felt they have endured injustice and violence for too long. Indecisive—because they knew that the fight for peace is a tough one, thus they were skeptical about whether to go into the fight or remain with the status quo.

Dear soldier, you are different. Your path to peace is a unique one. You know that this path will definitely lead to peace if you are patient and firm to the cause. Be strategic: move according to the rhythm of the enemy, but at every moment you have to remember that the objective is to win.

8. Speed in Other Sects

Speed is not a true Way of the Warrior

Musashi wrote that speed makes a warrior lose coordination and the flow of rhythm. According to him, it is bad to be too fast or too slow in anything. The warrior should see himself as an expert in swordsmanship, and an expert never does anything in a hurry.

Dear soldier, you know the true path of peace. You are the expert. Don't be in a haste. Your decision to restore peace means breaking down deep-rooted systems that have existed for centuries. It wouldn't be a walk in the park. The aim is to win—and winning takes precision, not speed.

There are times when the enemy would want you to be hasty so that you can mistakes. Do not lose your cool. Be calm. Don't let them draw you in. Take charge of the situation.

9. "Interior" and "Surface" in Other Sects

The way to understand is through experience

Other schools of swordsmanship classified their principles of swordsmanship into "interior" or "deep" principles, and "surface" principles. But Musashi disagreed with this. For him, he taught his students the Way of swordsmanship in a manner easy to understand. There was no need for rules or regulations, or classifying the lessons. For principles that were difficult to comprehend, he took time to explain them to his students according to their comprehension ability.

Soldier, you have the duty to educate others on the path of peace. But while you do that, do not hide anything from them. Explain to them why peace is important to the world. Show them the long history of chaos that the world has experienced. Then teach them why they should follow the soldier's path to peace. You are doing this because you know that there has been a lot of distorted information when it comes to the issue of peace. You have to tell a different story and change the narrative. By doing this, you erode the foundations of chaos that have already been built, and gradually enthrone the culture of peace.

Key Point from Musashi: *The sword does not have "depth" or "entrance" nor does it have a "supreme" posture. You only need your mind, and you also need to perfect the attitude of the sword. This is the nature of strategy.*

CHAPTER FIVE

THE VOID

In the Void

In Musashi's Scroll of The Void or Emptiness lies the secret for *perpetual* peace. Musashi believed that there is wisdom in believing that one does not know anything no matter how much one knows. When one accepts that they do not know everything, they increase their capacity to learn, to absorb more information. This is a place of nothingness, so there is enough room to be filled up with knowledge.

In this scroll, Musashi left some vital lessons for the warrior. And these lessons are also important for the soldier.

First Lesson: Musashi wanted the warrior to understand that even though he, Musashi, had shown him the true Way of swordsmanship, he should also be willing to learn more. The warrior should understand that learning the art of swordsmanship should not stop at reading *The Five Spheres*. The most interesting thing about the Scroll of the Void is that Musashi advised the warrior to also learn the way of other sects. I believe that Musashi did not give this counsel to the warrior so that the warrior could copy the way of other sects, but because of two reasons: (1) Since the warrior would be fighting samurais from other sects, he wanted him to learn their strategy—to know their strength and exploit their weakness. (2) He wanted the warrior to increase his own knowledge by understanding the way of other sects. After all, Musashi's Way of Strategy was birthed from observing and studying the way of others—and exploiting their weakness.

How does this apply to the soldier?
It is true that I have shown you exhaustively the true path of peace. But you should also understand that we live in a dynamic, ever-changing world. For this reason, you have to step into "nothingness"—the point of believing that you know nothing. This is why one of your qualities as a soldier is to be flexible as water. As you journey on this path to peace, be flexible to accept changes and adjust yourself to them without losing focus.

With the explosion of science and technology, you should know that the methods employed by the antagonists are bound not to stay the same. Just like we saw in the Wind scroll, it is important you move according to their rhythm. It is also important to focus on their mind, because that is the only way to predict their actions.

Learn everything that you can learn. Be open to new information. The internet is a vast place to gather information. Read. Listen. Understand. There are times when you would need to read or listen to information that is not line with your goal. But know that you are not consuming this information to be like the enemy, rather you are doing so because you want to get a peek into how the enemy thinks. You want to know their strength, their weaknesses. You want to know what they see as opportunities and what they consider threats.

The place of nothingness is a vast expanse. Do not limit yourself. As long as you keep your eyes on the goal, you are bound to win. Learn from Musashi: He learnt the ways of other schools, yet maintained his own Way of Strategy, and never deviated from it. And because of that he came out victorious, sixty-one times.

Lesson Two: Musashi taught his students in this scroll that they should never allow the true way to be tainted. They had the duty to preserve what they had learnt. In the beginning of *The Five Spheres*, Musashi noted that the true way of strategy had been abandoned. That was the primary reason he wrote *The Five Spheres*. And since he handed down his knowledge to his students, they had the duty to preserve it so that the true Way of Strategy would not fade away again. He wrote to them: *Never let the Way of the Warrior we practice to become tainted or obscured, not even a little bit. Your mind must never be lost.*

How does this apply to the soldier?
Dear soldier, you have learnt the true path to peace. Do not hoard it to yourself. Remember that the fight for peace is not one you can fight alone. To get other soldiers to join you, you have to educate them. You have to ensure that this path is neither tainted nor obscured. Use every channel possible to propagate this doctrine. Write books. Deliver speeches. Write

articles. Tweet. Let this message be heard around the world. Let it reverberate across the nations.

The duty rests on you to successfully transfer this message from generation to generation to generation. This is the only way the peace you fought for can be preserved. If the path of peace be lost, then the protagonists of violence may rise again, and when they do, it would be hard to defeat them again. Why? They have already seen all you've got.

Musashi said that the way of strategy must never be tainted or obscured, *not even a little bit*. I emphasized these five words because only a tiny loophole is needed for the ship of peace to sink. Let those you teach understand this. Let there be a oneness of mind, of knowledge, and of action.

Lesson Three: Musashi told the warrior that unless he understood the true Way, he would always look at human laws through the lens of right and wrong. But the true Way teaches him that human laws are a product of individual prejudices. They are distorted and as such go against the Way of the Warrior. This means that the warrior's swordsmanship cannot be based on human laws because they are already tainted and distorted. In the Way of the Warrior lies emptiness, and in emptiness, lies virtue, intellect, principles, and no evil.

How does this apply to the soldier?
There are human laws guiding human existence. And in most cases, the enemies of peace use these laws to suppress the rights of people. They use these laws to act out their violence, injustice, unfairness, and disregard for human lives. They wield the power to change the law as they see fit.

For instance, the Imperial War Museums recorded that there were "surprising" laws passed in Britain during the First Word War. The most important of these laws was the Defence of the Realm Act (DORA) which was passed to "secure public safety." But the constituents of the law didn't actually secure public safety but infringed on the rights of Britons. The law gave the government the power to prosecute anyone that acted in manner deemed to "jeopardise the success of the operations of His Majesty's forces or to assist the enemy." Some of its measures included: (1) banning whistling for London taxis in case it should be mistaken for an air raid warning, (2) forbidding people to loiter near bridges and tunnels or to light bonfires, (3) instituting the British Summer Time which made clocks go forward so that working hours in the day could be maximised, (4) introducing blackouts in certain towns and cities to protect against air raids, (5) censoring the press which limited the reporting of war news, (6) censoring private correspondence, and (7) restricting the movement of foreign nationals from enemy countries.[1] These laws show the extent the enemies of peace can go to limit the rights of individuals in order to promote their own agenda. In fact, one of the measures of DORA morphed into a restriction of food production which led to the introduction of rationing in 1918.[2]

This example shows the soldier that in many cases human laws do not favor peace. As Musashi rightly noted, these laws are promulgated based on human prejudices. So dear soldier, your only path to peace is the path which you know now. If you want to use human laws to your advantage, then you must find a way to become a lawmaker. And I don't consider this a bad thing. But I am skeptical about that because we have seen over time how power corrupts men and women. However, if you are certain that despite having and being in power, you would *always* follow the path of peace, then it is a good strategy. After all, the path of peace is also a path of nothingness, of flexibility, of applying knowledge geared towards peace.

Key Point from Musashi: *Train the eyes to perceive and see. There are no small clouds. You must understand that when the illusion clouds dissipate, then that is true "emptiness."*

A Practical Lesson From The Duel Between Miyamoto Musashi and Sasaki Kojiro[3]

The *Five Spheres* was not just a book of musings for Musashi, it was a documentation of the life he lived as a samurai. One duel that stamped Musashi's reputation as a warrior to be reckoned was his duel with Sasaki Kojiro that took place on the Ganryu Island on the 13th day of April, 1612.

Kojiro was considered one of the greatest samurais in Japan. He had *speed* and precision. His sword was a huge no-dachi blade that was *over a meter* in length. The size and weight of the blade made it a brutal weapon, but Kojiro perfected its use like no other samurai had done.[4]

Musashi, on the other hand, was a masterless samurai who was also well known in Japan. As at the time of the duel, Musashi had already sheathed his two katana and was only dueling with a bokken—a wooden practice sword.

On the day of the duel, Musashi arrived at the island three hours late. This infuriated Kojiro, who paced up and down with his hands behind his back. Kojiro was a man with a big ego and he felt Musashi's lateness was an insult to his honor. Three hours earlier, Kojiro was a calm man who even sat in deep mediation as he mentally prepared himself for the combat. It is said that his composure was so remarkable that his retinue of students and servants[5] had no doubt that he would defeat Musashi easily. But every element of composure and calm was lost as Musashi kept him waiting.

He grumbled, cursed and snapped at his servants. One of the officials tried to calm him down by telling him that there was a possibility that Musashi would not arrive because he had developed a weak feet thinking of the prospect of facing him. But Kojiro did not agree with this. He knew Musashi—he had a great reputation as a swordsman and wouldn't flee from a duel. And true to his thoughts, Musashi was just around the corner.

He sat cross-legged in a fishing boat not too far away from the island. As he sat in the boat, he, without haste, carved the boat's spare oar into a bokken with his sharp knife. After he was done, the fisherman rowed Musashi to the island.

When Kojiro saw Musashi, he was even more enraged by Musashi's appearance. Musashi was unshaven. He wore only a simple robe with a sword belt. His feet were bare. Also, he hadn't washed for some time because his robe had many stains and discolored patches. Musashi looked nothing like other samurais of the time. And Kojiro felt insulted by this.

He charged towards Musashi with his sword.[6] Musashi jumped and dodged to the left, and what happened next surprised

Kojiro. Musashi did not draw out a sword, but a bokken. A piece of wood.

Kojiro considered the arrogance that would make a samurai approach him with a wooden sword. This moment of consideration which led to further infuriation caused him to falter. He dived towards Musashi with a great sweep of his blade. Musashi ducked in time, with the sword cutting a wisp of his hair. Kojiro brought his sword down to Musashi again, but the latter evaded the blow. Musashi then stepped to the right and hit Kojiro's right side with his bokken. Then he struck another blow to the side of Kojiro's head. As Kojiro staggered, Musashi smashed the bokken into his left side. Kojiro felt his ribs crack, a sharp pain exploded in chest, and he couldn't breathe. The fight had ended as soon as it began. Musashi was victorious.

From this story, we see Musashi apply some of the tactics he later penned down in *The Five Spheres*. He knew that Kojiro had speed, and speed could make a samurai to stumble. Another thing Musashi knew was that Kojiro used an extra-long sword. This meant that although he was a skilled samurai, he depended on the length of his sword for victory—a tactic Musashi considered weak. But what is really striking about this story was Musashi's perception.

He knew Kojiro was a man with a big ego and he decided to use it against him. I believe he had watched Kojiro's duels and knew that Kojiro had great composure. So for him to defeat Kojiro, he had to get him agitated. Recall that Musashi advised warriors to take the opposite disposition of the enemy. If the enemy is calm, then the warrior should agitate him; and if the enemy fights in a hurry, the warrior should remain calm. For Musashi to get Kojiro agitated, he had to exploit his ego. Coming three hours late to the duel was an insult to Kojiro and because of that he lost his cool.

The moment Kojiro lost his temper was the moment Musashi gained victory. This is what Musashi called "Pulling the Bottom Out." He defeated the spirit of his opponent first before defeating him on the surface. Little wonder Musashi said that once a samurai understands the Way, he would remain undefeated. Through the Way—a mind game—Musashi defeated one of the greatest samurais with a wooden sword. Not even a katana.

Soldier, when you understand the disposition of your enemy, you would be able to use it to your advantage. Staying focused to the goal should be utmost in your mind. Kojiro was focused at first, but lost his focus because he allowed his ego override him. As a result, he fought with speed, no precision. That is why Musashi kept evading all his blows. And when the time was right, Musashi who had been *patient* all through, struck him hard and killed him.

PART II
WINNING WARS WITHOUT COMBAT

CHAPTER SIX
AN ALTERNATIVE APPROACH

The objective of every war is to win. No army engages in a war for fun except in war games. And even during war games, some heightened senses and actions imply that war is a serious affair. Indeed it is to kill or be killed, and for that reason, most battles and wars are fought to win. After all, victorious war veterans who live to tell war stories are celebrated while very few vanquished soldiers are ever heard of.

But wars are fought for more than just egotistical satisfaction. Of a truth, some conflicts are simply the products of the puppeteering expertise of highly placed politicians acting on their whims or the whims of *their* puppet masters.

Be that as it may, every soldier on the battlefield has one sole objective: to win. It is this objective that Musashi's Gospel is hinged on; defeating the enemy at all costs. Your country depends on it. Your loved ones depend on it. Most importantly, your pride and honor depend on it.

The last chapters you just read took you along the Way of the Warrior. You have been acquainted with the craft and guile of warfare, and you are now more aware of what it means to be a soldier defending the honor and pride of the fatherland. And as a human that has been trained to be a weapon, you are prepared and expected to commit the ultimate sacrifice to ensure that it happens if need be.

If anything, Musashi's Way of the Warrior and his life embody what the ultimate warrior should stand for.

Yet, if you have learned anything from Musashi's treatise on the use of the sword. From the way he draws the elements of Fire, Water, Wind, and Air into the discourse of the Warrior's Way and his emphasis on entering into that space known as the Void, you should have noticed that there are multiple ways to win a war.

This part of the book will deal with the ability to win a war with minimal (where possible, zero) physical combat.

Could There Be War Without Physical Combat?
Yes, it is possible. Avid students of politics and economics will regale you with never-ending tales of instances where countries and groups of partnering countries have allowed divergent interests to reflect in their international policies. The Cold War of the 1980s comes to mind, and more recently, the US-China trade wars are examples of politico-economic wars that have not escalated into full-blown military wars.

These situations can be mentioned in a discourse of this context because most military wars are products of political and economic aspirations. The soldier on the battlefield is a vehicle or device for realizing these aspirations to all intents and purposes. To borrow a quote from Niccolo Machiavelli's *The Prince*," The acquired kingdoms were conquered by either fortune or the talent displayed by the ruler's army or by a foreign army."

There is a salient question if the soldier must make economic aspirations a reality using blood, sweat, and tears as the currency for achieving said aspirations. This question stems from a conflation of different positions, which are:

1. The need to win wars at all costs using blood, sweat, and tears where possible
2. The soldier's desire to live as long as possible (self-preservation is an inalienable human drive)

If these positions are part of the dynamics of war, then the question arises, "Is it possible to win a war without physical combat? Better put, is it possible to win wars with minimal expenditure of blood, sweat, tears, and everything else in between?

War has been likened to the game of chess. And even in chess games, pawns are sacrificed to protect the queen, the most important chess piece on a player's side of the board. So if pawns are sacrificed to win games (read wars), does it follow that soldiers must always pay the ultimate sacrifice for wars to be won?

These are the questions that this section of the book will explore. Exploring these questions is particularly important given the frightening military might that most of the world's powers boast of.

On The Virtue of Emptiness

To explore an alternative means to winning wars, you'd need to be willing to explore that chthonic space which Musashi describes as the "Void" or "Emptiness."

This concept describes a place that exists beyond human knowledge and understanding. It refers to a realm of ideas where you can create anything because of the flexibility and formlessness that it affords everyone that has access to it.

Embracing the realm of emptiness lends the ultimate warrior the tools required to explore previously unknown options. This capability makes creating an alternative approach to winning wars possible.

How, might you ask?
Well, here is the thing, the ultimate warrior (that's you) must be proficient in using weapons of warfare as he is with his mental faculties. Thus, the soldier who understands the Way of the Warrior understands the importance of a constantly sharpened mind and is willing to master as many strategies as the mind can handle.

To Musashi, the partnership between a sharpened mind and a resolute will offers entry into the realm of the Void, where free yet disciplined thought leads you to a world of immense possibilities for creating the right strategies.

Indeed, you will be walking a path less trodden as you'd be free of the illusions that impair the perception and reasoning of so many a soldier. Illusions can becloud the very senses required to be successful at war.

Yet like clouds, illusions must dissipate at a point. It is at this point of dissipation of the clouds that clarity comes. This is why Musashi likens the Way of the Warrior to the cloud because of the constant transformative process of cloud forming water before falling as rain, only to gather back as a cloud at the appointed time.

Musashi aptly describes the virtue of 'Emptiness' in *The Five Spheres* thus:

In emptiness is virtue, and there is no evil. In emptiness, intellect exists. Principle exists. The Way exists. And the spirit is nothingness.

Once you have grasped the concept of 'Emptiness,' enter into a realm of being that predisposes you to take the form required to achieve your immediate goal.

This understanding takes us to the next milestone on your newfound path to victory with minimal physical combat.

Preparation

A mind that has embraced the void of nothingness is open to new things. To walk the less-traveled path known as The Way of the Warrior, you need to prepare your being for a revolutionary approach that takes your enemy by surprise. After all, what is the point of using strategies and ways of warfare that are common knowledge and could be easily countered?

To prepare yourself to achieve your ultimate goal as a warrior, your mind is your ultimate weapon. Indeed planning and preparation require a reset of your old ways of warfare. We live in a digitalized world. Military equipment has evolved from swords and spears to fully computerized equipment that consists of software that controls the military equipment (hardware).

Think of your mind as software and your physical body as the hardware. Your mind determines what your body does, and when the mind is at its best, the body follows suit. Musashi puts it as clear as day when he notes:

Develop a large mind — a mind like water. Depending on the situation, the mind should be flexible like water. Water can be dark blue. It can be a drop or a vast ocean.

When your mind takes the property of water, it is able to adjust to the situation. And to win a war with minimal combat, you'd need to be flexible enough to adapt to any situation that might arise. He who walks through unchartered areas has to be willing to align his path to the contours that he encounters along the way.

Understanding As A Means of Preparation
Why is it essential for a soldier to understand anything beyond military strategies and perhaps how to make the most of his weapons? The answer to that is this: understanding the nature of warfare is the difference between losing and winning a war. You need to master the "traditional" tenets of war before creating yours.

All the most outstanding scholars and strategists all have one thing in common. They studied the ideas and principles propounded by the great minds before using these ideas as a foundation for theirs. As the ultimate warrior, you'd need to understand the five "determinants" of war as propounded by Sun Wu.

The first of the five is the concept of Righteousness. Sun Wu sees righteousness as the means of making people "willing to join with the king, to make them unite and join forces, to live and die with courage."

We have already established that you are the sword of the king—the vehicle through which his will is realized. Your engagement in battle is born of your conviction that you are doing the right thing. This conviction will come in handy at those points in your where doubt might set in because of the uniqueness of your approach to winning with minimal combat.

The next determinant is the Atmosphere. Sun Wu defines this as "the night or day, hotness or coldness, and change of four seasons." Your battles will have physical locations, all of which are subject to the Atmosphere. Traditional war strategists have a perspective on the seasons and have created tactics based on these seasons. Your ability to perceive the failings and strengths in their tactics will help you formulate an approach that sets you apart.

The terrain is the third determinant, and to Sun Wu, it is the "high or low ground, near or far distance, easy or difficult roads, plains or canyons and the conditions of survival." We will call this the physical location of the battles you will engage in. If you are going to win your opponent with the least physical combat possible, you will need a level of mastery of your terrain. You'd need to understand how the terrain works in your favor or against you. The ideal is to win a war and live to tell the story. Why else would you be looking to win with minimal physical combat? Understanding the terrain is key to coming up with strategies that put your enemies in disadvantaged situations. Afghanistan is a prime example of how physical terrains affect warfare. The relationship between its unique terrain and the fatalities experienced by the Coalition forces, who were unfamiliar with the terrain, is well documented.

The General is the next determinant in Sun Wu's list. Vu believes that he must be "strategic, trustworthy, kind, courageous and strict." These are the characteristics of the ultimate warrior. You can't win the war against your enemies if you haven't won the war against yourself. Having these values puts you in a better situation to make the right decisions that help you achieve your ultimate winning goal.

Martial law is the fifth and last determinant which he who chooses to walk the Way of the Warrior must understand. Martial law in this regard refers to the "organization, management of soldiers and expenditures in the military."

The organization is very important in the military as it provides the structure needed to implement a strategy. For an army to be organized, its soldiers must be well-managed. Managing soldiers also requires the proper handling of the available resources. You must be a "professional" student of martial law, one who is constantly improving on his body of knowledge about keeping his soldiers in the right frame of mind at all times.

Understanding Sun Wu's war determinants prepare you to explore alternative paths to winning wars. Mastery of these factors provides the foundation for building your unique strategies and tactics. To facilitate your understanding of his ideas, Sun Wu listed several situations that you must consider at each point in time:

- Which party has the righteous king?
- Which party has the talented general?
- Which party benefits more from the atmosphere and terrain?
- Which party abides by martial law?
- Which party owns the better, more sophisticated weapons?
- Which party's soldiers train more frequently?
- Which party rewards and punishes more fairly?

The soldier who is prepared for all has the advantage over his counterpart is limited to the traditional ways of warfare. Preparation allows you to make the most of situations as they arise instead of being hedged in the box. Understanding the nature of war is essential to your preparation.

The Nature of War

War takes place on multiple levels, primarily as physical and psychological combat that often involves firepower, troop strength, morale, leadership, courage, effective decision-making, and tactics designed to handle battlefield and non-battlefield situations. Regardless of its form, in the context of this work, war is essentially some form of military combat between two or more parties.

War is strictly distinguished by its scope and goal as typified by the clash of major interests backed by the parties involved. To this end, we would refer to war as sustained (or not) combat between trained soldiers who represent political or economic interests.

It often involved using military forces that attacked enemy soldiers and designated points, appropriated geographical locations, or gathered intelligence. With wars, information, tactics, and strategies are employed to achieve often mutually exclusive goals. Ultimately, an intricate web of interactions must be effectively managed to achieve victory.

One of the most common reasons for war is the enforcer of political will, where clashing political interests quickly degenerate to physical combat. This is the most common form for which a soldier is expected to die for the "honor" of the country. Although there are both defenders and aggressors in this dynamic, both sides of the conflict believe they are in the right, and victory is often seen as a non-negotiable outcome. This approach to warfare leads to sustained effort, expenditure, and mostly irreversible and large-scale destruction.

Indeed, it would seem as if warfare is a primordial aspect of man's existence. Indeed, all of the political states that exist today were created and sustained by wars. Either one state is trying to protect or defend social, religious, or political interests from both internal and external aggressors. History is replete with examples of wars from pre-literate times to the present day.

The Evolution of Warfare
Just as man has experienced physiological, social, and technological evolutions over decades, war has also significantly evolved both in nature and dimension.

The modern age has seen the proliferation of wars between state and non-state actors where guerilla groups with personal and political interests have engaged states within and without state borders. Yet again, the modern age has experienced wars where nuclear weapons capable of destroying multitudes have changed the paradigms of warfare.

Political states now use these weapons and the threat of using them to achieve their goals or prevent bullying from other political states. The pissing contest between the US, China, Iran, and North Korea comes to mind. Of a truth, nuclear weapons have revolutionized warfare in modern times as countries could "easily" obliterate each other with the touch of a button without the need for combat between soldiers.

That said, the proliferation of nuclear weapons appears to be a double-edged sword. One side of the blade is the instant destruction of the earth, while the other side of the blade ensures the nuclear powers exert some restraint.

But modern wars have evolved beyond the weapons used. We are now entering a phase in civilization where technological advancements (namely robotics and artificial intelligence) will soon eliminate the need for armed humans in wars. The United States has already started deploying robots and drones to handle tasks hitherto done by humans: disarming bombs, detecting threats, performing reconnaissance, and firing missiles.

Even military robots and drones are being designed to be deployed in combat areas adjudged to be too dangerous for humans. This is as biological engineers actively seek to eliminate the need for traditional weapons and armies. They have taken their studies to the point where certain human vulnerabilities are being targeted for improvement or replacement. On the flip side, there is talk of bioweapons like a bio-engineered virus being used in place of nuclear weapons in the future—cyber warfare, where the internet and its minions will be used as a weapon of warfare.

To all intent and purpose, man's wars gradually evolve into bloodless combat between non-human actors (read soldiers). Yet again, regardless of its nature or form, war at its simplest is an expression of a conflict of interests.

Understanding Your Place In Contemporary War
Obviously, we are slowly moving towards the kind of warfare that requires little or no physical combat, all thanks to technological advancements. Yet we are not there yet, as contemporary warfare is yet to catch up to the futurist wars captured in many sci-fi movie flicks on Netflix and Amazon Prime.

This is for you who seek to elevate your "warriorhood" to the highest levels possible. You have a lot to learn from the quintessential warrior Miyamoto Musashi who won all the duels he partook in.

Winning that many duels over the years was only made possible by his approach to combat, which was hinged on minimal dependence on physical strength against reliance on technique, strategy, and all the other intangible aspects of warfare. In situations where the surprise was needed, Musashi employed it. When the strategy was the difference-maker, he used it to his advantage. Yet again, the emotional manipulation of his opponents was another tool in his bag of tricks, just as the mastery of his combat skills was another.

Musashi's secret was to go above and beyond the capabilities of his opponents. Where they relied on training, flashy weapons, and battle-tested tactics and techniques, Musashi explored the Void, grasping the power of responding at the moment and adopting a fluid strategy that handled whatever came up.

As you prepare for war, myths, misconceptions, and traditional tactics and strategies must be archived. Because that is where they belong, you'd need a different strategy that is as fluid as water yet as effective as steel. Winning wars does not require a hard and fast formula; instead, the essence is to explore all the possibilities that lie in the realm of the Void. As much as your strategy is vital, it must be creative, fluid, and fitting.

CHAPTER SEVEN

MILITARY STRATEGY

No one can truly follow the Warriors Way without understanding the way strategy. Miyamoto Musashi won so many duels because he was strategic about everything. From his mastery and use of his sword strokes to how he studied his opponent's emotions and used them to his advantage.

Strategy is critical in conventional warfare. It is doubly critical when you are looking to win your battles and wars with minimal physical combat. To get a grasp of strategy and its place in Musashi's teachings, we'd be looking at how strategy in warfare evolved over the years.

What Is Military Strategy
As the name suggests, military strategy refers to how military campaigns are planned and coordinated to achieve military objectives. Military strategy is reflected in the tactics that an army applies in battle. Let's put things in perspective. Strategy is the way a set of battles are used to win a battle and is often seen in how the troops are used in combat.

The success or loss of any battle or war boils down to the strategy used. We find evidence of this fact in the Greek origin of the word *strategos*, which roughly translates as "the general's art." Every ardent student of war history will observe that despite the influence of technology on military strategy, at its root, military strategy refers to the way military operations are managed to achieve defined objectives.

Military strategy is designed to handle specific issues that often arise in and out of the theatre of war and is often limited by the size, training, and morale of forces on the ground. It is also affected by the grade and number of weapons used, the terrain, the weather, and how well trained the enemy forces are. Now that we have established military strategy let's look at how it evolved over centuries.

Military Strategy Over the Years
We could trace the beginning of military strategy to the growth and expansions of political empires worldwide. Some of the notable names in the development include Philip II (382–336 BC), Alexander the Great (356–323 BC), and Hannibal (247–183 BC), all of whom made innovations in their approach to warfare long before Musashi discovered the secret of the Warrior's Way.

Philip II found a way to merge infantry, cavalry, and artillery into a proficient fighting unit that could be easily be manoeuvred where and when necessary. Alexander the Great is one of history's most accomplished strategists and tacticians. He earned this reputation by being particular about planning, communication, supplies, security, and the element of surprise.

Hannibal used flexible attack tactics, unity of command, and an elite cavalry that laid the ground for developing the Roman military strategy that made them some of the most successful armies of all time.

What we know as modern warfare started with the exploits of Gustav II Adolf, king of Sweden (r. 1611-32). Adolf brought back maneuver into military strategy by having a national army structured into small, well-armed, and easily maneuverable fighting units.

Perhaps Frederick II (the Great) of Prussia (r. 1740-86) made the most significant changes in military strategy over the years. To make the most of the challenges he faced at the time, Frederick II used interior lines and a highly disciplined army and horse artillery that he could easily assemble where he wanted to strike his enemies at different points.

Napoleon, I structured his military campaigns so that he could easily maneuver his troops to focus on different battlefields. His battle approach included skirmishing, cannonading, and a great concentration of forces adept at turning and enveloping battlefield maneuvers. It is safe to say that Napoleon heralded the beginning of modern military strategy as his tactics became templates for many army generals that came after him.

By the 19th century, military strategy was again modified by technological changes in the volume, reach, and speed of warfare. Military equipment expanded and improved, so there was a change in the tactics and strategy. Take the U.S. Civil War, for example, where the North and the Confederates fought over political interests. The victory of the North can be linked to a strategy that includes several tactics like the blocking, division, and destruction of the Confederate armies and supplies.

When machine guns and airpower were introduced into war dynamics, the military strategy took another turn. War generals moved from trench warfare to strategic airstrikes on cities and enemy positions. These airstrikes, in particular, greatly changed the face of modern military strategy and warfare. A few well-trained pilots with the latest fighter aircraft could wreak more havoc in less time than even the most advanced ground soldiers could.

Perhaps that is when the first seed of the idea of optimized combat results with minimal physical effort was sown. Because warfare soon moved from fighter jets to nuclear bombs that could obliterate countries with just the push of a button from a remote location. With almost every technologically advanced country owning nuclear weapons, military strategy has further evolved. For one, it engendered some level of responsibility among world leaders who are somehow aware of nuclear weapons' destructive potential. Seeing as none of these leaders value world annihilation over their political interests, military tactics have been forced to adjust to meet the prevailing sociopolitical conditions.

Warfare is now being executed mainly by small, elite forces that have training in guerrilla war and are equipped with state-of-the-art, light weapons that facilitate speedy deployment and withdrawal to and fro enemy lines.

Musashi on Military Strategy

One thing that is clear in our summary of the history of military strategy is the significance of maneuverability to the success of military campaigns. Like we mentioned at the beginning of this chapter, Musashi's unprecedented win ratio in his sword duels is down to his approach to strategy.

In his words, *"when you attain the Way of strategy, there will not be one thing you cannot see."*

If you want to experience as many wins as a soldier in modern warfare, you'd need a great understanding of military strategy. Here are some other insights from Musashi:

"The way to win in a battle according to military science is to know the rhythms of the specific opponents and use rhythms that your opponents do not expect, producing formless rhythms from rhythms of wisdom...Cultivate the power of insights; if strong, the state of affairs in everything will be visible to you."

Musashi's book is a bestselling eclectic treatise that is currently a source of instruction in several fields of thought because the majority of the chapters in the book focus on how you can gain leverage over your enemies. Coming from a place of experience(what with so many wins), Musashi's firsthand experience with strategy is evident in how he tries to show soldiers how to win as many wars as possible using the correct strategic principles.

One of such principles is the need to learn as much as possible, even if it is one's enemy that one has to learn from. The reason is even the most loathsome enemy is not without strengths. To Musashi, learning from such an enemy is a great strategy.

For one, studying your enemies' habits, strengths, and rhythms enables you to arrive at unexpected winning strategies that put you in a favorable position to win your battles. It is a lot easier these days with all the technological advancements that we currently enjoy.

The idea is to mine as many insights from your study of your enemy. The higher the quality of the insights, the better you arrive at a really great strategy because you get to see the battle from their perspective. Once you understand your enemy's view on a battle, you are better positioned to arrive at countermeasures and counter-tactics that give all the advantages that you need.

As counterintuitive as it is to study your enemy, it is an effective approach that you don't want to write off because it gives you one of the most critical advantages that you could ever take advantage of timing:

"Strike fast when you realize the opportunity. Do not flinch your attention at the point, and your opponent will not be able to react. Mow him right down without even giving him time to blink his eyes."

Timing is of the essence in most things in life, especially combat situations. It is a vital cog in any military strategy as knowing when to strike or retreat is key and is the difference between a successful and failed military campaign. Many major battles have been lost because one of the parties missed their opportunity to strike.

But studying your enemy is not as easy as it seems. Mushasi believes that:

"When opponents come at you, appear weak at first, then overcome him...The important thing in strategy is to suppress the enemy's useful actions but allow his useless actions."

You'd need to master some subterfuge when dealing with your enemy. As a master strategist, you must be steps ahead of your enemies. And to do that, you must be willing to adjust your tactics to match the demands of the environment or any pressing situation. Disinformation might be a necessary tactic when you discover the need to throw your opponent off their position of power. For instance, you might need to respond to attacks by feigning weakness, after which you attack at the right time.

Another instance of disinformation is trying to convince the enemy that you will be doing one when you will do another. This tactic could be deployed by calculatingly letting out information so that the enemy believes that the source of information is authentic and that they got a "scoop." The thing with this tactic is that it could lead the enemy to waste resources on "useless actions" when deployed correctly. One real-life illustration is in the third world war.

At a point in the war when they needed to launch their D-day invasion, the Allied forces had to use deception to mask the launch of their major offensive. As part of the ruse, General Patton was given command of a landing force comprised of airfields, dummy tanks, landing craft, oil storage depots, and airfields. All of these things were done in full view of the German spies and military command.

The Allies then proceeded to bomb the Calais region when the Normandy area was the real target of their attack. They used their double agents to relay the wrong information while fabricating radio traffic that sold the illusion that a large invasion force was being assembled in the southeastern region of England. The Allies executed these measures so well that the Germans could not deploy their troops effectively to counter the Allies' attacks.

Why Is Strategy Important To You?
The focus of this part of the book is winning wars with minimal physical effort. To this end, having a clear and focused strategy goes a long way in the success of this approach to conflict. For one, you'd be taking an uncharted path, and so the pitfall to be experienced are more, and the potential for failure is higher. Without a well-thought military strategy, you are almost likely to fail.

On the flip side, you have everything to gain if you find a way to create a strategy that prepares for all the eventualities that might arise at each point. To Musashi, "*The principle of strategy is having one thing, to know ten thousand things because it is important to see distant things as if they were close and to take a detached view of close things.*"

But all that mastery and understanding of things outside come to nothing without self-mastery. That is why self-mastery is the first step to effective military strategy. Musashi succinctly describes it thus *"Study strategy over the years and achieve the spirit of the warrior. Today is victory over yourself of yesterday; tomorrow is your victory over lesser men."*

Why Use Strategy
"...a skillful leader does not need to use the battlefield to subdue the enemy. He captures the enemy's city without having to attack. He destroys enemy countries without putting his troops in great risk. All is to preserve the force by making use of strategy. Therefore, there is no wear and tear, and still, there is great benefit. This is the strategy of offensive art..." -Sun Wu.

(The Law of War: The Art of Competition Benefits in War, Business and Life)

You could simultaneously fight a war on two levels: the psychological and the physical. Psychological warfare is targeted at the will of an army, while physical warfare tends to affect the capabilities of your foes. When applied correctly, numerical and weaponry advantages are removed, and the war is won at less human and material costs.

Any military leader worth their onions will incorporate attack levels in their strategy because both the physical and psychological work is in tandem for a soldier to function optimally. A fitting analogy would be to see the psychological side as software that powers a hardware component (the physical side)

For the rest of this section of the book, we will use the word "will" interchangeably with the psyche while "capability will refer to the physical. Now that that's out of the way, let's look at physical-based and psycho-centric strategies that could be used to win a war.

Physical-Based Strategies

These are strategies targeted at the physical or tangible aspects of warfare.

Executing Physical Damage

One of the targets of war is to inflict as much physical damage as possible on the enemy. It often involves physical violence as a means of annihilating the enemy. The sustained annihilation of one's colleagues at arms has a debilitating effect on the capability of even the most motivated soldier.

Granted, inflicting physical damage on an army has led to many wins, but the context of this treatise is to seek alternative means of winning a war with minimal body bags being flown home.

If inflicting damage is a surefire means of winning a war, then a difficult question arises 'What is the number of soldiers an enemy has to lose before they concede defeat? In some instances, soldiers on a battlefield lay down their weapons and either flee or surrender when they conclude that a battle has been lost.

One might be tricked into labeling such soldiers cowardly and disloyal in discharging their duty to defend and protect. However, the number of dead soldiers and the rate at which they are killed will disorient many soldiers and cause them to save their lives first.

Thankfully, the destruction of an army does not have to come from the death of soldiers. Most modern armies are greatly enhanced by the quality and caliber of their weaponry, so a lot of modern military strategy is often based on these weapons.

Naturally, it follows that getting rid of these weapons will greatly affect the enemy's tactics and strategy and give you the upper hand. There is ample evidence of wars that have been won using this strategy, right from the Boer Wars in South Africa through the Arab-Israeli Wars to the Taliban's deft maneuvering in Afghanistan a few months back. The destruction of enemy weaponry and structure has always been a viable tactic for winning wars with minimal human casualties.

Effecting Disruption
This is yet another military tactic that works like a charm when used right. Every army is based on the efficiency of its structure, where different parts function as a whole. The disruption of a military organization renders the organization ineffective even when there is no physical loss or death of the organization's members. The attack is targeted at the structure and not the humans involved in running the organization.

Disruption can occur in an army's organization by surprising them or executing one's operations faster than they expect. Taking action before the enemy will affect how effective their response to any attack is, and this could lead to complete paralysis of the enemy army's organizational structure. A thoroughly startled army will not implement any tactics properly, nor will it defend its positions well.

The element of surprise can be a great ally once you are ready to decide and implement your actions as soon as possible. However, you would need to avoid hastiness in your bid to execute your actions faster than your enemy. You must be prepared and sure of your actions, or you will lose the element of surprise when initiating action.

Evasive Tactics
Another tactic is using evasive tactics, where you carry out military operations so that the enemy can't put the finger on your tactics or strategy. The principle behind this strategy is that it is difficult to defend and attack every position effectively. Therefore, when you attack the enemy through positions that they are not prepared for, they are forced to scuttle any plans they have, which could disrupt their tactics.

You might also choose to attack the enemy in areas where they do not have the manpower to defend effectively or counter your attack. The principle behind the evasive strategy is to scuttle whatever formation or tactics that the rival army might have. When done properly, the enemy's forces will be disrupted, and you could be a step closer to victory over them. A prime example is the hit-and-run tactics.

Guerilla warfare is a prime example of evasive tactics, and it has been effectively used to destroy powerful armies throughout history.

This strategy is hinged on short, unexpected attacks and a lot of maneuvering that allows the attackers to withdraw and avoid engaging the enemy. It has been used to expose and weaken enemy defenses before the enemy can respond in force.

Attacks by Special Forces units and terrorists are some of the more recent examples, although this tactic finds expression in the Lusitanian War, the Battle of Manzikert, the Battle of Ain Jalut, the Turkish War of Independence, the French and Indian Wars, the Vietnam War, the Soviet-Afghan War and America's recently abandoned military campaign in Afghanistan. All of these wars saw smaller armies forcing their larger enemies into tactical disadvantages using guerilla warfare.

Breaking Communication and Logistic Lines
This is a strategy where you target the communication system of the enemy army. We have already established that an army needs a fully functional and cohesive structure to operate. This structure is built and maintained via open lines of communication.

One of the best ways to break up an army's structure is to cut its lines of communication. When reports and commands along the army's hierarchy are not fully communicated, it becomes difficult to arrive at a clear picture of the situation. Consequently, it becomes difficult to formulate a strategy or even the tactics needed to attack or defend.

It becomes easy for you to isolate and attack your enemy positions because they cannot call for support since you have severed lines of communication. This strategy is often effected by jamming radio frequencies, cutting wires or capturing messengers. You could also achieve the same result by deliberately dis-informing the enemy by feeding them inaccurate information that will negatively affect the reports and the orders issued so that things are tilted in your favor. Another angle of disinformation is to cause resentment within the rank and file of the enemy's army via wrong information that puts the sender(s) and the recipient(s) at loggerheads.

Once you can break up the lines of communication, you increase the chances of disruption and ultimately a loss of cohesion and effectiveness in the army.

You could also opt to sever the transportation lines that link different divisions/units of a military campaign. The transportation routes are just as important as communication lines because they provide support, reinforcements, and supplies to each unit.

There are always points/areas between these units that make them vulnerable to attack. Once you can block the communication and logistic lines between these units, you limit the movement of supplies and reinforcements, which are essential to the success of any military campaign.

This strategy has always played out in military conflicts for a while now. During World War II, cargo ships containing much-needed supplies were targeted and sunk. The German Navy couldn't sink as many ships as the Allied Forces, and so Britain was able to keep a supply chain on the Mediterranean Sea. Consequently, this allowed the Nazis to be attacked from North Africa, and it significantly affected the outcome of the war.

In the Battle of Ilomantsi, the Finnish forces were outgunned and outmanned by the Soviets. However, their successful attacks on Soviet supply lines forced the Soviets to retreat, leaving valuable military equipment in the process.

Eliminating a Key Player/Component
An army is an organization with multiple components working cohesively. Yet a key player or component keeps the structure functioning optimally. This concept is not limited to a human factor, but it includes any part of the military campaign vital to its success.

The key player in the human context could be the general in charge of the military campaign, some of his trusted lieutenants, the elite forces, or even the head of state. You could also target key equipment and infrastructure significant to the military campaign, like destroying airfields and key military bases, nullifying vital codes, or blowing up train tracks or key roads.

Psycho-Centric Strategies
"In doing battle . . . you achieve victory by irregular means. So if you are good at irregular warfare, you will be as inexhaustible as the sky and the earth."-Sun Wu.

If the enemy's capability is the hardware and his mind is the software, you could affect the software so that the hardware no longer functions. The mind is more potent than most military strategists acknowledge, and so you'd be entering uncharted territory when you opt to explore ways of affecting your enemy's psyche.

Psycho-centric strategies are designed to break the enemy's will to fight and oftentimes win him over to your side. Like most military strategies, it has its roots in pre-modern warfare.

Genghis Khan is one of the most popular of that era. He was exceptionally skilled at instilling fear in the hearts of his enemies by spreading rumors about the vicious Mongol horsemen in his army. He was known to have his soldiers carry three lit torches at night to suggest numerical strength. He also had a reputation for catapulting severed human heads over the walls of enemy settlements as a shock tactic.

During WWI, armies used planes to drop flyers and non-lethal artillery rounds behind enemy lines as a means of spreading propaganda. The German and Allied Forces had units that specialized in psychological warfare, which they used in WWII. Both sides also used radio broadcasts to their advantage. The Nazis and their allies, the Japanese, used radio broadcasts like "Axis Sally" and "Tokyo Rose" to spread false information about their victories to demoralize the Allied Forces. The Americans were able to one-up them with their play at "leaking" false orders that deceived the German high command into preparing for an Allied invasion at the wrong location.

ISIS (one of the more recent terrorist organizations) employs social media and other online platforms to implement psychological campaigns calculated at currying support and recruiting fighters from all over the world.

Let's look at some techniques that strategists have designed to reduce the enemy's will and help you win the war with fewer body bags.

Causing the Enemy To Lose Confidence in Themselves
Constantly failing at something has a dampening effect on anyone's psyche. Soldiers at the battlefront have to go through very dehumanizing, mind-altering situations which task the mind even after retirement. It is one thing to win a battle after going through those brutal conditions after achieving the goal.

It can be devastating when an army has to go through these harsh conditions and still lose battle after battle. After a while, the soldiers start to lose confidence in their abilities, no matter how well trained or equipped. Once the soldiers' morale is low, they no longer have the will or zeal to fight.

Ever heard the saying, "It's not the size of the dog in the fight but the size of the fight in the dog ?" Roughly translated, this means that the will to fight is the critical factor in winning any fight, battle, or war.

The power of the will is the singular reason why wars are won and lost.

It is also the secret behind rag-tag armies and guerillas holding their own against fully trained, well-organized armies. Find ways to cause losses to the enemy's military campaign, even if it is as small as an attack on their communication and transport lines or supplies. As long as you inflict the losses inflicted strategically, it will start to tell on their psyche after a while.

Sometimes you could even strategically use disinformation to create an appearance of defeat to achieve a loss of confidence in the enemy's need for the military campaign. Most military forces take the time to compute the cost of resources expended and their casualties. And even when such information is on a need-to-know basis, word always gets out, and in those instances where the information is less than great, it will dampen the soldiers' morale. You could opt for this technique to sow the wrong ideas in the enemy.

Effecting a Loss of Confidence in the Military Campaign
A loss of confidence in one's ability as a soldier will degenerate into a loss of interest in the military campaign. The reason for this is simple. After sustained losses, soldiers tend to lack motivation and ultimately see the military campaign as needless and wasteful exercise, especially when they feel that the losses are a high cost to pay for whatever interests the way might be pursuing.

Most military commanders understand this fact. That is why they are constantly looking for ways to improve the soldiers' morale before, during, and after battles. The aim of attacking the enemy's mind is to get them to review the losses that have been inflicted on them in terms of the results. In situations where the losses do not seem to match the promised results, there will be a loss of confidence in the need for the war.

Soldiers are programmed to die for something: defending their homeland or protecting it from external aggression. For example, look at the furor that the loss of American soldiers in Somalia, Iraq, and Afghanistan caused and see how it affected those military campaigns. A military strategist who can manipulate the enemy's mind to lose motivation and doubt the validation of a military campaign has won half of the war.

How?

Most times, this loss of interest in the war often goes beyond some disgruntled murmurs in trenches and at gatherings of soldiers. The loss of interest can degenerate into large-scale desertion of soldiers or even full-scale mutiny that could threaten the lives of the commanding officers. An army's military might depend on discipline and organization. Once that is lost, the soldiers are nothing more than a group of armed men with little or no direction or purpose. These minute things deteriorate to the stage where you could easily pick them off. Or even co-opt them into your military campaign, which is a win-win situation by all means.

Which Approach Is The Best?

It all depends on your approach to the war. Are you looking to achieve a hard and fast destruction of the enemy's military equipment? If yes, then that would require specific, concentrated, and concerted efforts to get things done as soon as possible. It is essentially an all-or-nothing approach to warfare.

Physical-based strategies target the speedy destruction of the enemy or its equipment and all. It is based on the principle that the swift destruction of the enemy's military strength is the fastest way to end the war with minimal damage. Military strategists who subscribe to this approach to warfare believe that eliminating the enemy's strengths will cause a collapse of the enemy's forces and lead to surrender or defeat. Sadly, many physical-based strategies do not always work if the advantage of military might is not there. You'd be in a suicidal situation if you opted to go all out against an enemy that has more soldiers and more military hardware than you. The sheer difference in numbers will defeat your aim of winning the war with minimal casualties.

Psycho-centric strategies apply a progressive approach to winning away. Attacking the enemy's will to fight is a gradual process that takes time. It is based on the principle that attacking the enemy's will to fight can lead to a surrender of enemy forces with minimal losses for the protagonist. Now, while there are fewer casualties with this approach, it takes time and is just as complex.

The reason for this complexity is that it often depends on the situation and the key players' ability to execute the plans as effectively as possible. Another downside is that an enemy that is the wiser to your antics can outmaneuver you and use your tactics against you.

So which approach works best for a military strategist who intends to win the war with as few casualties as possible? This question recognizes the fact warfare is dynamic, and the results of a well-planned war are often light-years apart from the projections on the drawing board.

The best approach is to blend both systems to arrive at what we would term as the 'Ultimate Strategy'.

The Ultimate Strategy

Mushasi captures the need for an ultimate strategy when he submits that:

"In strategy, it is important to see distant things as if they were close and to take a distanced view of close things."

A distanced view of close things involves an objective approach to handling issues. Here is where you step out of the immediate situation to get a better view of the state of things. Call it thinking out of the box, if you will but what Musashi is trying to say is that your approach to strategy should be different from most and, by extension, unpredictable. Hence "...see distant things as if they were close and to take a distanced view of close things."

Taking such an approach to strategy makes you flexible and difficult to anticipate. Your enemy does not know what strategy you might deploy and if you can alternate your moves mid-campaign. For instance, destroying the enemy's manpower and equipment might cause a defeat or a surrender if properly executed, and certain situations work in your favor. But in some cases, with the right amount of destruction of the enemy's forces or sustained disruption of its military operations, you could achieve the same effect.

In such an instance, there is a blend of physical-based strategy and the psycho-centric strategy. The sustained destruction of the enemy forces and their equipment was an example of a physical-based attack on an army's physical capabilities. At the same time, the disruption of their military operations via sabotaging their preparations and lines of communication and supplies and destroying vital components is an aspect of the psycho-centric strategy.

The psycho-centric approach aims to convince the enemy that a loss is inevitable based on past and current experiences. If he wins by some odd twist of fate, it would be a pyrrhic victory that he'd be hard-pressed to justify.

For Sun Wu, achieving a flawless victory in a military campaign is inseparable from great strategy:

"Military strategy is like flowing water. The characteristic of water is to avoid high places but drain into low places. So, victory in the war is due to avoiding strong enemy positions attacking weak enemy positions. Water depends on the terrain to adapt. Combat depends on the enemy's situation to arrange. So there is nothing certain in war as the water never holds a certain form."

(*The Law of War: The Art of Competition Benefits in War, Business and Life*)

However, Sun Wu only recommends the destruction of the enemy's army after attacks on the opponent's strategy and diplomacy to destroy its alliances have failed.

His ideas are further reinforced by the thoughts of Niccolo Machiavelli thus:

"…you must know that there are two kinds of combat: one with laws, the other with force. The first proper to man, the second to beasts, but because the first is often not enough, one must have recourse to the second. Therefore it is necessary for a prince to know well how to use the beast and the man. Thus, since a prince is compelled of necessity to know well how to use the beast, he should pick the fox and the lion because the lion does not defend itself from snares, and the fox does not defend itself from wolves. So one needs to be a fox to recognize snares and a lion to frighten wolves."

— *The Prince: Chapter XVIII*

In sum, these great minds believe that you have to deploy a balanced strategy that is flexible enough to adapt to situations yet powerful enough to achieve the desired result. Military commanders have had to change the way they operate in the field. But to do that, you need to be in a state of calm amid the chaos around you.

The Power of a Calm Mind

Military combat has an ugly aspect to it. Such is the horror of this violent yet primordial facet of human reality that our consciousness is affected whenever we are involved in violence. It doesn't matter if we dispense or receive it; the outcome is the same; some measure of stress is generated.

Now stress wreaks havoc on the brain. Humans (and indeed all animals) are wired by nature to protect themselves in the face of danger. It is an unconscious and automatic reflex. So whenever we are in dangerous situations, our bodies secrete stress hormones like cortisol and adrenaline. Once these hormones get into the system, they put us in a state where we either fight or run from danger.

That wouldn't be so bad if it were not for the physiological reactions that come with these biochemical reactions. Some of these reactions include a faster heart rate, a trembling solar plexus, sweaty palms, a constricted throat, a rigid jawline, a tightening of the back of the neck, and shallow breathing, and we breathe in more oxygen. Many combatants have experienced this set of reactions at one point. The best of them are those who have mastered the ability to calm their minds even when their bodies are stressed.

For most people, even soldiers, it becomes difficult to make complex decisions, which can be dangerous for soldiers at war. All that is important is how to deal with the imminent danger. Interestingly this response to stress is meant to be a short-lived one.

The reason is that all that cortisol that is pumped into the body starts to take a toll. And so, after a while, one's health starts to deteriorate. But most importantly for soldiers, stress affects decision-making, which is vital in creating and executing an effective military strategy.

The reason is that stress narrows the focus to oneself and possible survival and prevents you from seeing the big picture. You can easily observe more in a less stressful situation, and you find it easier to communicate better. When you are in a calmer state, you manage your energy better, your mind is clearer, and you focus better. You are ultimately more productive, creative and you are more innovative.

Most military organizations focused on hardening the bodies of their soldiers and improving their proficiency in the use of weapons and the execution of tactics. Drawing from the analogy we used earlier in this book, the focus has been on making the hardware better.

Thankfully that is changing. There is now a focus on the mind and its ability to be trained like a muscle. There is a trend in modern military training that sees training the mind as a means of improving soldiers' performances on and off theatres of war. The new catchword is "mindfulness": a crucial part of modern military training.

Mastering the Art of Mindfulness
"If you correct your mind, the rest of your life will fall into place"
-Lao Tzu.

Mindfulness is known to offer a range of benefits, including enhanced mood, immune function, attention, and pain tolerance, among others. It is also known to decrease stress while heightening cognitive functioning. Interestingly, the practice of mindfulness has been introduced into military training. This is due to the recognition of its potential to enhance soldiers' performance on and off theaters of war. Interestingly, the concept of mindfulness is central to belief systems that promote peace and oppose conflict. Yet soldiers are using mindfulness practices as tools to help them manage the stress and attendant trauma that is part and parcel of warfare.

So what exactly is mindfulness?
Well, simply put, the idea of mindfulness training refers to practices that train the brain to remain in the present. Folks who have mastered the art of mindfulness can relax, lower

their blood pressure, enjoy better sleep, become more focused and alert, optimize their motor functions and improve their relationships.

Why Is Mindfulness Important For Soldiers
For soldiers, in particular, mindfulness training improves their abilities to perform at their best when off-duty, during drills, and in a theater of combat. It is also used to decrease pain, stress, and trauma that is associated with post-deployment and post-traumatic stress disorder (PTSD). Soldiers also use it to enhance their impulse control.

Mindfulness training makes it easier to enhance one's ability to pay attention to the present moment while acknowledging your current emotions, thoughts, and sensations evenly and without bias. It efficiently eliminates issues like mind-wandering, worrying, and trying to appraise the past. With mindfulness, you have tunnel vision that is focused on the present so that you don't get distracted from current events. You simply accept your current reality without any judgment.

The good thing about mindfulness is that it is a skill, and like all other skills, it is transferable and can easily be acquired. Better still, you get better at it the more you practice you put into it. Once you can find the time to practice mindfulness regularly, you will get better at reducing your impulse to get triggered by stressful situations. At the same time, you get better at maximizing your awareness, concentration, and decision-making. That way, you make better decisions; you are more proactive and less reactive.

During drills, soldiers who practice mindfulness find it easier to be safe when trying out new drills. Their memories are sharper, so they can remember even the most challenging tests and qualifications like shooting drills and other important training exercises. These drills are designed to put them in real-life situations and help develop the ability to eliminate distractions while handling their mind-body management of performance anxiety is crucial to their ability to perform in theatres of combat efficiently.

Mindfulness also helps improve situational awareness, which is vital in combat situations. For example, a soldier who is given to a mind-wandering will not be aware of his environment or the particular situation he finds himself in. In addition, appraising situations with bias or judgment will generate the kind of stimuli that affects your ability to optimize the resources you need to execute tasks, prevent disaster, or promptly and effectively respond to crisis situations.

Soldiers will be less lethal and less resourceful during combat situations if their minds keep wandering and they find it difficult to focus on a situation fully. With practical mindfulness training (no matter how short) for even relatively short periods (for example, 8 hours over eight weeks), soldiers will have better focus and improved situational awareness. They will also be better equipped to tolerate the different combat environments (Volatile, Uncertain, Complex, and Ambiguous) that they might encounter during a military campaign. So with well-honed skills, they can respond to stimuli appropriately. Such soldiers will also have a higher pain threshold than others outside the mindfulness training.

But mindfulness practices are not all about dealing with combat situations. There will be "dwell times" when soldiers are off-duty. This is when soldiers create bonds, and friendships are cultivated. A soldier who cannot handle the stress and trauma of warfare will have poor interpersonal relations and will often be isolated even in battle because they lack the right connection with other soldiers.

On the flip side, clients who take mindfulness training will be able to build and maintain productive relationships with colleagues and loved ones. They also find it easier to relax and de-stress themselves.

Mindfulness training is particularly important during intensive training periods before deployment. This is a crucial period because soldiers are being physically and psychologically prepared for getting into stress-prone and potentially dangerous situations. In addition, mindfulness training imbibes the training better and makes them better soldiers in real-time combat situations.

Several studies (notably at the University of Miami and the University of California, San Diego School of Medicine, and Naval Health Research Center) have carried out mindfulness studies on American soldiers. For example, the study at the University of Miami revealed that mindfulness training facilitated the attention span of soldiers, prevented mind-wandering, and could improve cognitive abilities.

The study at the University of California revealed that soldiers who practiced mindfulness techniques could cope with the demands of combat situations a whole lot better than those who didn't.

Why Mindfulness is Crucial For The Ultimate Warrior
Mushasi is believed to have never lost any of the 72 duels he fought in his lifetime. Besides being a master of martial arts, he was a master of his mind. He was an unalloyed proponent of meditation, and he is known to have used his knowledge in his fights.

Musashi's mastery of mind and matter should be the blueprint for the modern-day soldier looking to walk the Way of the Warrior. Let's put things in perspective for a minute. How was it possible for Musashi to defeat tens of warriors, some of whom were younger, stronger, faster, and more skilled than him?

Baring the use of magic (black or white), such a feat could only have been possible if he knew when his opponents would move before they did. That would mean that he had a strategy that was flexible, efficient, and, most importantly, challenging to counter. Creating and executing such a strategy would require some mastery of the mind, and we would be safe to assume that he practiced some form of mindfulness or the other. His thoughts on the "Void" lend credence to our assumption.

"Your mind must never be lost…Polish the twofold spirit of your mind and your will."

These are words on marble for every modern warrior. You need to step out of the box that has led most soldiers to believe that they only need hard bodies and quick fingers to stay alive during the war. Step into Mushasi's void and let this mental space provide the clarity of thought and purpose you need to avoid being one of the body bags on the next flight home.

As a commander of men responsible for the success of combat missions and the lives of the men under you, mindfulness is non-negotiable for you. There are times when things will never go as planned, no matter how many consultations and plans are made on the drawing board. There will also be times when the success of a mission and low casualties will become mutually exclusive. Tons of other distractions would threaten your decision-making at crucial points during a military campaign.

It would be best if you stayed calm in the face of conflict. Your life and the lives of your men depend on that. Being in control of your mind long enough to see things for what they are without an iota of bias or judgment is the difference between an effective military strategy and a botched one that leads to casualties.

Being mindful is key to your strategy as the Ultimate Warrior. In Mushasi's words:

"Think accurately and clearly. Think big. Develop the "empty" nature in your strategy."

CHAPTER EIGHT

THE WARRIOR AND THE ETHICS OF WARFARE

War takes a toll on even the most emotionally detached warrior with iron-clad self-mastery. After seeing enough bloodshed for a while, you start to wonder if it is all worth it after all. You might even begin to question the rationale behind large-scale bloodletting. Is war obligatory? If yes, how then should it be staged?

The thrust of this treatise is winning a war with minimal casualties on your side while inflicting maximum casualties on the enemy. One begins to wonder at the means to achieve that goal. Are drones and long-range missiles considered ethical means for achieving these goals? What about distinguishing between enemy combatants and non-combatants. More so, is death the only signifier of defeat?

Miyamoto Musashi is famed for winning about 60 life-or-death duels by the time he was 29. Yet it is believed that at a point, he stopped killing his opponents as he entered the duels with a wooden staff with which he attacked until the opponent tapped out. Moreover, he did this even when his opponents intended to kill him or cause grievous bodily harm, at the very least.

One can deduce that Miyamoto's change of "tools" (for want of a better term) signaled his change in perspective about the goal of combat. Of course, one can argue that he was tired of the bloodletting that often comes with such duels, but even that in itself shows that he saw combat differently at that point. Indeed, the bulk of his writings was about winning with the least loss possible and for that perception to materialize in the choice of a wooden staff in armed combat suggests one thing: the application of ethics to combat.

According to Musashi, the warrior's path is paved by discipline, focus, restraint, and honor and is maintained by moral and ethical codes. One could draw parallels in his philosophy to the Just War Theory advanced by St. Augustine in the 5th Century and St. Thomas in the 13th Century.

Two of the more popular concepts in this theory," Jus ad Bellum" and "Jus in Bello," which mean "the reasons for going to war" and "the conduct of war", respectively, describe wars as ethical or unethical. Based on the Just War theory, a war was deemed ethical when it was waged by a legitimate authority that fought for a just cause and with the right intentions. Such a war was often the last resort and should be deemed as a last resort when every attempt at dialogue fails. It is also expected that in an ethical war, there had to be discrimination between combatants and non-combatants.

In reality, modern warfare straddles this description because there are a lot of wars that have been waged using unethical means like drones, landmines, torture, and chemicals. There are also a plethora of instances where both enemy combatants and non-combatants have been killed in a war, especially when the use of military force was deemed "disproportional" to the scope of the war.

Machiavelli advanced the opinion that princes gained and kept power by waging wars, and going by the growing tensions between Russia and the rest of the EU, wars might not end anytime soon. However, we might yet see a situation where both sides of a war attempt to achieve a bloodless victory.

Does Just War Theory Count in PostModern Warfare
There is an aspect of Just War theory that deals with the corpus of rules or agreements like the Geneva and Hague conventions structured to delimit the kinds of warfare that were deemed "acceptable." Interestingly, these agreements are subject to religious beliefs, race, and language differences. When both sides of a war see each other as subhuman because of these differences, ethics of war rarely apply. Just War theory will rarely apply in the genocidal wars that have been waged across continents. Yet warfare has always been influenced by rules of engagement. At the time, several codes of warfare prevented attacks on non-combatants like children and women. In addition, there was some sense of "honor" that made it "unsoldierly" to participate in certain acts of war. That is not to say that these codes were always subscribed to giving the accounts of the activities of the Teutonic Barbarians, Vikings, Huns, and the Mongols(of the Gengis Khan era), among others.

Because

"You must know that there are two kinds of combat: one with laws, the other with force. The first is proper to man, the second to beasts, but because the first is often not enough, one must have recourse to the second."

Niccolo Machiavelli, *The Prince*

Indeed the current narrative of the efficacy of the Just War theory in promoting the codes of warfare is an interesting one. On the one hand, there is an increased awareness of the need to get soldiers to imbibe the tenets of Just War theory. On the other hand, interestingly, more military academies create courses around the justification of war and its application.

Sadly, that has not put an end to war crimes as genocidal campaigns are still on the rise, just as extremist attacks have become the new normal in some parts of the world.

So does Just War Theory matter in postmodern warfare? To answer that question, we'd need to take a look at the theory and the concepts upon which it is built.

The Concept of Jus Ad Bellum and PostModern Warfare

Jus Ad Bellum is built on the idea that a just war must be fought for a just cause; it must be a last resort and be instigated by a legitimate authority. It must also be informed by the right intention and be most likely to be successful using proportional means. Now, these tenets might be definite, but it affords some level of flexibility to their application as all of the tenets are relative and could be interpreted based on the context of the situation.

The Idea of Just Cause

What could be considered a just cause in a war between opposing parties? Each side of a war that is the recipient of an act of aggression would term retaliatory attacks just, seeing as the right to self-defense is an inalienable human right. To this end, it is difficult to define what "just cause" means in the event of a physical and mental injury, trade embargoes, perceived slights, and the appropriation of a state's boundaries.

Let's take, for example, the conflict between Russia and the EU over Ukraine's decision to become a member of NATO. Clearly, both sides of the conflict have legitimate arguments. Ukraine has the right of association, while the Russians might have adopted their stance because of the economic and political implications of such a move by Ukraine. If both sides perceive the achievements of their interests to be of utmost priority, it would be difficult to argue that neither of them is acting unjustly.

So going by Russia's relatively unprovoked bombing of Ukraine, Ukraine will be morally justified to launch its attacks. And going by the prescriptions of Just War theory, *both* sides will be justified to pursue such a campaign. Defensive reaction to physical force (anticipated and implemented) can be justified to all intents and purposes as long as the acts of war are implemented to prevent or retaliate against aggression from external aggressors.

This leads us to the question, "Is it justified to launch the first attack to prevent a war. Again, in the illustration of the Russia/

Ukraine imbroglio, is it justifiable for any of the parties to launch an attack in the belief that it could forestall a full-blown war?

Will any of both sides be justified if they borrow a leaf from this submission:

"There is no avoiding war, it can only be postponed to the advantage of your enemy." Niccolò Machiavelli.

This submission leads us to the next tenet:

War as the Last Resort
Wars have ripple effects that often takes a while to correct. And so, war should only be used when other options are off the table.

Proper Authority
The concept of proper authority revolves around the belief in the state's sovereign power. Yet, arriving at such a position is problematic because not all declarations of war that are seemingly accountable and legitimate really are. Certain military policies and campaigns pursued by these countries might not be justifiable. Indeed more modern societies have developed the ability to walk that space that is influenced by the political forces of sovereignty, accountability, and necessity.

Right Intention
The tenet of right intentions is hinged on the belief that wars should be waged to pursue just causes and not because of selfish interests. So in a sense, a pursuit of a national interest via war might be termed unjust.

This might be a bit problematic in itself. Earlier in this book, we established that most wars are extensions of political interests that are often mutually exclusive. In this context, such wars will be termed selfish and unjust. Consequently, gauging the right intentions is tricky because intentions are relative, and what might be right in one content might be wrong in another. So what one person sees as the right intentions might be the wrong intention to the person on the other side of the war. For example, both sides of the Russia/Ukraine crisis can claim to be pursuing the standoff because they both have the right intentions.

Reasonable Success
This is yet another problematic tenet in Just War theory. It suggests that a war should not be waged until it is absolutely clear that the possibility of winning is high. So in such an instance, the pros and cons of a military campaign need to be ascertained before such a campaign can be launched. Going by this submission, the US military campaigns in Vietnam, Iraq, and Afghanistan can be deemed unjust.

However, while this tenet and approach to warfare might be deemed practical and even realistic, there are existentialist issues that it does not cater to: "Would it be right to refuse to defend one's territory because the chances of success are low" "Would it also be right to refuse to seize the opportunity to obliterate an enemy when the opportunity presents itself."

Proportional Means
This tenet straddles the ethical aspects of warfare. It deals with how wars should be waged and states that a war is just

when the means used to win a war are proportional. More like don't bring a gun to a knife fight or a tank to a gunfight. To understand this tenet, let's put things in perspective first. Let us say that Russia invades Ukraine with tanks and soldiers. Now, if/when Ukraine decides to counter-attack, it must never embark on its campaign using nuclear weapons. The idea is to even out the attacks on both sides. If Ukraine hypothetically attacks with a nuclear weapon and Russia survives, there will be yet another round of attacks. But if Ukraine were to respond with proportionate weapons, Russia won't feel that they have been one-upped, and the conflict could reach a logical end.

The Case Against *Jus Ad Belum*
The principles of *Jus ad Bellum* we just described provide pointers towards revisiting military ethics. There are quite some problematic issues in the principles largely because of their open-ended nature that supports multiple interpretations. Given that war is a complex and relative affair, the Jus Ad Belum concept might not completely cover all the angles of the discourse on military ethics. However, it provides a foundation for our understanding of what it means to apply ethics to military warfare.

However, the brutal character and devastating scope of postmodern warfare of war despite the codes of warfare, the prominence of Just War theory across different fields, and its impartation in military academies are telling. History is replete with examples of the brutality of modern warfare, from the bombing of civilian centers in Germany and Japan through the dropping of nuclear bombs on Hiroshima and Nagasaki to the bombing of Ukraine by Russia in the first quarter of 2022.

It would seem like ethics and war might be unmixable because they represent two ends of a stick that could never meet. However, from our description of the principles of the *Jus Ad Belum*, it is clear that nine times out of ten, existential realities (manifested as political interests and military necessities) would always displace the issues of ethics in warfare. Heck, the very nature of warfare makes the discussion of ethics and morals a needless exercise.

That said, the warrior looking to walk the Path and make his own path within that Path must understand the balance that an understanding of the ethics of warfare lends him. And to get a better understanding of the ideas contained in Just War theory, we will be looking at the *Jus In Bello* concept and its relation with postmodern warfare.

Jus In Bello and PostModern Warfare

With the *Jus in Bello* concept, which deals with "just" conduct in warfare, there are three tenets upon which this concept is built: Discrimination, Proportionality, and Responsibility. The tenet of discrimination assumes that there are legitimate targets of warfare, while the tenet proportionality deals with the amount of military force considered ethically appropriate. Finally, the tenet of responsibility focuses on where the responsibilities of the warring parties lie in warfare.

The Principle of Discrimination

Going by the *Jus in Bello* concept, indiscriminate attacks are considered unjust because the non-combatants are not considered legitimate participants in the war and are expected to be excluded from the theatre of war. This is based on the assumption that these parties, by virtue of their existence and activities, are not active in the business of war which is essentially the killing of combatant soldiers.

A perfect analogy for this situation is boxing. It is a crime to throw a punch at someone going about their business of life. Yet anyone who steps into a boxing ring is by virtue of that space assumed to be in a situation where it is legitimately acceptable to throw and receive punches.

Combatants in war are in the same situation. Based on their training, dressing code, and their bearing of arms, they are in a space where it is acceptable by the codes of warfare to kill or be killed: whether their duties are combative or not. On the other hand, it is assumed that non-combatants do not have this status. As such, waging war on unarmed and untrained persons is considered by the principle of discrimination to be an illegitimate activity. This also extends to surrendered soldiers or soldiers turned civilians who have laid down their arms and are no longer active in warfare.

The Principle of Proportionality

> *"Do not fight but subdue the people."*
> Lao Tzu *The Book of Ethics*

This principle assumes that combat-related action must be proportional to the objective of the action. It is similar to the same tenet of *Jus Ad Belum* except that for *Jus In Bello*, the extent and violence of warfare is modified to minimize destruction and casualties. It essentially seeks to reduce overall while doing the right thing regarding the level of force that is appropriate in a war.

Of a truth, there will be the possibility of the wrong kind of military force being used against combatants in a war. Military history is replete have been instances where combatants have been killed even after they have surrendered, just as there are instances where non-combatants have been killed in the course of a war.

Does the proportionality principle raise questions about the concept of highly selective killing or assassination? The idea behind such killing is that such specific killing of key threats to peace and stability and war crime criminals as long as such targets are legitimate.

To a large extent, it would make a lot of sense if a legitimate target is killed to avoid further bloodshed or further the objectives of a military campaign. The tendency of such a form of attack generates a chain of retaliatory attacks of the same nature, just as it could be applied in other spheres of human interactions.

The Principle Of Responsibility
The *Jus in Bello* concept advances that soldiers in a war should be held accountable for their actions. It is morally permission for combatants to kill their counterparts to a large extent. However, it becomes an act of irresponsibility when a combatant knowingly opens fire on non-combatants or pursues fleeing soldiers for the thrill of it. Such acts will lose the legitimacy of warfare and enter the realm of war crimes.

The tenet of responsibility is linked to the tenets of the *Jus ad Bellum* and *Jus in Bello* because some measure of responsibility informs the nature of wartime activities. There have always been instances of soldiers going against orders from higher-ups because obeying such orders went against their sense of responsibility.

While this might be a drop in an ocean of barbaric attacks executed in the name of war, it serves as a model for the modern warrior who seeks his path on the Way of the Warrior.

Such a warrior is guided by an internal compass built from the highest values. That is the only way to prevent being consumed by the deepest depravity that is often kindled by acts of war.

The Case Against *Jus In Bello*

> *"Do not fight but subdue the people."*
> Lao Tzu *The Book of Ethics*

That would be the right path to follow in an ideal world. But a soldier on the war front has little or no time remembering the principles of discrimination, proportionality, and responsibility with the combination of the cacophony of gunshots, the surge of adrenaline, and the overwhelming drive to stay alive. Now that is the scenario of symmetrical warfare where it is soldier versus soldier. Applying Musashi's admonitions of keeping it mind over matter both in and out of the theatre of combat becomes extremely difficult.

It is even more difficult when fighting in less regular situations where one has direct interactions with a civilian population of supposed non-combatants that provide cover for the enemy. For example, American soldiers in Vietnam, Iran, Iraq, and Afghanistan have often had situations where they were done in by a civilian population that appeared may not have borne arms but were actively in support of the enemy.

The concept of *Jus In Bello* is further challenged by modern weaponry and the change in military strategies that have been occasioned by the asymmetrical warfare that has become the order of the day.

Jus Postbellum

Where the soldiers stomped, the thorns grew there.
After winning big battle, there must be a crop failure.
Lao Tzu *The Book of Ethics*

At the end of every war, one of three things happens: the army is either defeated, victorious, or has agreed to a truce. Regardless of the outcome, things are never the same before the war. That is where the last and least popular concept of the Just War theory (*Jus Post Bellum*) comes to play.

Jus Post Bellum is pertinent to any scenarios that play out in the aftermath of a war. It is expected to show some amount of graciousness to the vanquished. Non-combatants should not be punished even as their rights or traditions should not be trampled on. It is also worth considering the rehabilitation of the vanquished.

It is important to treat the aftermath of a war delicate because

"It is important to remember that there is nothing more difficult to solve and more dangerous than the adventure of creating a new regime."
Niccolo Machiavelli *The Prince*

One never has to be soft or hard, or you risk making more dangerous enemies than you started with. Therefore it is important to avoid exploiting the conquered politically or economically. Now, although the thesis of Jus Post Bellum is the ethical handling of a vanquished side regardless of its enemy status before the war, it bears repetition to note that you must tread carefully at this point because rehabilitating the vanquished side might lead to unwitting humiliation and the provocation of a burning desire to revenge.

Yet, a ruthless approach to the situation might generate the same results.

Ethics and the Concept of Bloodless Wars
Conducting a war has a saying:
One does not dare to be a master
But just want to be a guest
One does not dare to advance one inch
But just wants to take a foot back
That is advancing without contest
Set a battle without having to raise your arm
Capture the enemy without having to use a weapon
Lao Tzu *The Book of Ethics*

There is so much technological advancement that it would take a lot to implement the concept of a bloodless war truly. For example, there are so many remote, precision weapons that might ensure the safety of an army's ground forces. But what happens when the army has the same military might and can easily launch effective remote attacks. For instance, let's say both armies have access to the latest toys on the market: drones.

Drones have become the latest addition to the "bloodless" philosophy of modern warfare. They are believed to be affordable, and they eliminate the possibility of a drone-wielding army losing a lot of its soldiers. Drones are remotely controlled by pilots who don't have to see combat firsthand, so the war might be "bloodless" for them, but what about the victims of the drone strikes?

In the recent war between Armenia and Azerbaijan, many of the victims of drone warfare were non-combatant civilians. This raises moral and ethical issues regarding the incidence of war and its consequences. If the idea of a bloodless war is to minimize heavy military casualties, what is the rationale for killing non-actors in the armed conflict? However, in wars fought between standard armies and insurgents without high-tech weapons, some insurgents often evade or launch attacks using the local civilian population.

There is so much technological advancement that it would take a lot to truly implement the concept of bloodless war. For example, there are so many remote, precision weapons that might ensure the safety of an army's ground forces. But what happens when the army has the same military might and can easily launch effective remote attacks. On the flip side, there are bound to be casualties on the other side.

Except there is a move in the military space to replace human soldiers with robots. That might be the level of warfare where we have bloodless wars. Until we get to that point, we will still have to find ways to marry the ideal of bloodless wars with our current realities, if that is ever possible.

To achieve a semblance of that union, the human factor will have to come into play. Essentially, we will need a stronger application of a universal code by which armies across the world conduct war.

The Need for a Code
Regardless of the changing face of warfare, one constant is that humans play vital roles in and out of it. Technology and equipment aside, war is essentially the attempt at using any form of violence to get another party to submit to your will. It is one of the most selfish endeavors because while it aims at getting another to submit, you are simultaneously trying to maintain and possibly, improve your sovereignty.

The current realities of war as we know it is constantly shape-shifting, hence the need to keep one other constant: codes. There are both written and unwritten codes for combat that have guided combat over the years. But all of those are universal external codes that are only effective to the point at which the individual practices them. It is different with a different set of codes and personal convictions that, after all, is said and done,

ON THE SOLDIER'S PATH

drive the individual's thoughts, words, and ultimately actions in and out of combat theatres.

We emphasize the importance of personal convictions because, as popular as the Chivalric codes of the time, there were many casualties during the Medieval era. And a significant number of these casualties were non-combatants. Moreover, over the years, there were changes in these codes (ostensibly for the better) to match the changes in technology and consciousness.

Yet, what we know as war crimes persist (they may not have been seen as that during man's darker, bestial days), howbeit on a different scale.

Be that as it may, to Musashi, the modern warrior exists for one reason:

"The only reason a warrior is alive is to fight, and the only reason a warrior fights is to win. Otherwise, why be a warrior? It is easier to count beads."

So as long as there are legitimate sovereign states with often mutually exclusive interests, there will always be soldiers like you to protect and preserve those interests. And where there are soldiers, wars are inevitable. Yet to Lao Tzu:

"Weapon is an ominous tool. Gentlemen don't use it. Only used for reluctance."

This takes us back to Musashi's position about mastery over the mind as the ultimate weapon. Knowing when and how to use your military training is the essence of a soldier who seeks the way. If you are in a war to win, then the best path would be to take actions subject to moral conditions. After all, if war is to be waged as a last resort meant to prevent a worse outcome, why be reckless with the power that you wield?

As a soldier in the current military space, you'd need a clearer understanding of the power of your mind to be able to win wars with minimal casualties. When you get to the level where you can pick your fights on your terms with the right strategy, the war is half won.

Being able to control and apply your mind, which happens to be your greatest weapon, makes the difference between if you become a casualty of the war or if you live to tell war stories as a war veteran in your senior years. The key lies in the codes that you live by.

We are in one of the most technologically advanced epochs of our time. We have reached heights that most folks could only have been dreamed about a few decades back. However, our advancements have proven to be a double-edged sword that has also caused us harm concerning the devastating character of the global military space. We have reached the crossroads where we realize that there has to be a paradigm shift as far as our wars go. Or else we risk global self-annihilation.

Thankfully, the thoughts and teachings of great minds like Niccolo Machiavelli, Lao Tzu, and Miyamoto Musashi provide a Way out for the modern warrior. But knowing about the path is one thing; staying dedicated to that path is another. With constant re-evaluation and restrategizing, it is possible to win wars with minimal casualties. It will only require a dedication to master oneself and to make that persistent mastery over self a religion:

"*Today is victory over yourself of yesterday; tomorrow is your victory over lesser men.*"

Miyamoto Musashi

CONCLUSION

There is an interesting twist to the duel between Musashi and Kojiro. Although Musashi was victorious, tears dropped from his eyes as the fisherman rowed him away from the island. He had just defeated—destroyed—one of the greatest samurais in the land, and he didn't see the purpose in doing that.

For Musashi, he didn't gain anything from the victory, but the land had lost a great warrior because of him. Musashi believed that Kojiro had a lot to offer to swordsmanship because his skill as a swordsman had been honed from years of experience. And all that was gone because he, Musashi, had killed him in a pointless duel.

Musashi continued to study and teach swordsmanship, but he never killed an opponent in a duel again.

Dear soldier, I have written the concluding part of Musashi-Kojiro's duel as the concluding part of this book because I want to let you know that restoring peace has a purpose. Unlike Musashi who took out a great samurai from Japan, you are adding something great, something valuable to the world by restoring peace.

This is the point where there is a little contrast between you and Musashi. Musashi cried because he regretted his victory, but you would rejoice when you gain victory. It is said that when Kojiro died, his retinue of servants, students, friends, and officials rushed towards Musashi to attack him but he was gone before they could get him. Yours would be different: On the day you win this fight for peace, many would rush towards you, not to attack you, but to praise you and thank you for bringing to them what they have desired all along.

When this happens, know that it is your chance to share the knowledge you have gained. Know that it is your chance to ensure that the path of peace is not tainted or obscured. Seize the opportunity to propagate everything you know. Teach them to always follow the map. To be soft as water. To be fierce as fire. To be enigmatic as the wind. And to step into the void.

NOTES

PART I: THE FIVE SPHERES

CHAPTER ONE: EARTH
Follow the Map

1. The katana has been an iconic symbol of Japanese Samurai tradition since the 13th century. It is a curved blade of up to 37 inches long with a single cutting edge that faces outward. The katana consists of a handle (Tsuka), pommel (Kashira), handguard (Tsuba), and a lacquered wooden scabbard (Saya).
Source: "How the Katana Sword Became a Symbol of Samurai Tradition." www.invaluable.com/blog/katana-sword/. Accessed 1 October 2020.
2. "Samurai Swords." www.angelfire.com/dragon/swords/katana.html. Accessed 1 October 2020.
3. The wakizashi is a curved, single-edged blade between 12 and 24 inches long. It is smaller than the katana and offers more ease in close combat fighting. It was also used to behead the defeated opponent.
Source: "Samurai Swords: The Wakizashi." *Swords of the East,* www.swordsoftheeast.com/wakizashi-swords.aspx. Accessed 1 October 2020.

4. The wakizashi was used to perform the ritual suicide known as *seppuku*. This ritual was carried out by a warrior who felt that they were living in great shame by disappointing their master or by being humiliated in one way or another. Source: "Samurai Swords." www.angelfire.com/dragon/swords/katana.html. Accessed 1 October 2020.
5. "Samurai Swords: The Wakizashi." *Swords of the East*, www.swordsoftheeast.com/wakizashi-swords.aspx. Accessed 1 October 2020.
6. "The History of Japanese Daisho." www.martialartswords.com/blogs/articles/the-history-of-japanese-daisho. Accessed 1 October 2020.
7. Martin Kelly. "5 Key Causes of World War 1." *ThoughtCo*, 26 March 2020.
8. Blake Stilwell. "The 7 most notorious traitors in military history." *We Are The Mighty*, www.wearethemighty.com/amp/the-7-most-notorious-traitors-in-military-history-2554876440. 6 December 2017.
9. Barack Obama. "Remarks by the President in Address to the Nation on Syria." Office of the Press Secretary, The White House, 10 September 2013. www.obamawhitehouse.archives.gov/the-press-office/2013/09/10/remarks-president-address-nation-syria. Accessed 6 October 2020.
10. ibid
11. "Vietnam War." *History*, www.history.com/.amp/topics/vietnam-war/vietnam-war-history. Accessed 6 October 2020.
12. ibid
13. Cynthia M. Grabo. "Strategic Warning: The Problem of Timing." *Central Intelligence Agency*, 2 July 1996.
14. The first date selected by Hitler for the attack was 12th November 1939, but he didn't attack until 10th May 1940. Source: ibid

15. ibid
16. Between 2007 and 2017, British cyclist won 178 world championships, 66 Olympic or Paralympic gold medals, and 5 Tour de France victories.
Source: James Clear. *Atomic Habits*. New York: Penguin Random House LLC, 2018. E-book

CHAPTER TWO: WATER
Soft As Water

1. "The Worst War Crimes Ever Imaginable." *All That's Interesting*, https://allthatsinteresting.com/worst-war-crimes-in-history/, 2 June 2016. Accessed 12 October 2020.
2. Two declassified government documents reveal that the United States paid over $2.3 million for the data. The United States also used research gained from Nazi experimentation to improve their own biological warfare program.
Source: ibid
3. One of the women, Masika Katsuva, recounting her ordeal to filmmaker Fiona Lloyd-Davies, said that she and her two daughters were raped. Her husband was murdered in front of her, and she was forced to eat his genitalia.
Source: ibid

CHAPTER THREE: FIRE
Fierce as Fire

1. Kennedy Hickman. "Wars and Battles Throughout History." *ThoughtCo*, 14 January 2020.
2. Books also destroyed included the works of 1929 Nobel laureate, Thomas Mann, a German author whose critique of fascism angered the Nazis; Erich Maria Remarque, whose description of war in her book *All Quiet on the Western*

Front was considered "a literary betrayal of the soldiers of the World War"; and Helen Keller, who believed in social justice and championed pacifism, women's voting rights, improved conditions for industrial workers, and the disabled. Works by German literary critics like Erich Kästner, Heinrich Mann, Ernst Gläser; American authors, Jack London and Theodore Dreiser; and Jewish authors, Franz Werfel, Max Brod, and Stefan Zweig were also affected. Source: Holocaust Encyclopedia. "Book Burning." *United States Holocaust Memorial Museum.*
3. United States Holocaust Memorial Museum. "Nazi Book Burning." *YouTube.* https://youtu.be/yHzM1gXaiVo.
4. ibid
5. Julie McCarthy. "Why Rights Groups Worry About The Philippines' New Anti-Terrorism Law." *npr*, 21 July 2020. https://www.npr.org/2020/07/21/893019057/why-rights-groups-worry-about-the-philippines-new-anti-terrorism-law. Accessed 20 October 2020.
6. ibid

CHAPTER FOUR: WIND
Enigmatic as the Wind
1. Bassam Aramin faced similar criticisms from the Palestinians. All they wanted was the lingering enmity between Palestine and Israel. But for Bassam, Rami, and others who understood the path of peace, they knew that "it is not a decree of faith that we should live forever with a sword in our hands." Source: Colum McCann. *Apeirogon.* New York: Random House, 2020. E-book.
2. ibid
3. ibid

CHAPTER FIVE: THE VOID
In the Void

1. Source: Imperial War Museums. "10 Surprising Laws Passed During The First World War." www.iwm.org.uk/history/10-surprising-laws-passed-during-the-first-world-war. Accessed 22 October 2020.
2. Other measures included in DORA were regulating the opening times of pubs and reducing alcohol strength, making the possession of cocaine or opium by anyone other than authorized professionals a criminal offence, and issuing fines for making white flour instead of whole wheat and for allowing rats to invade wheat stores.
Source: ibid
3. Jack Beckett. "A Turning Point In The Life Of Musashi, The Undefeated Samurai." *War History Online*, www.warhistoryonline.com/ancient-history/turning-point-samuraimusashi.html. Accessed 23 October 2020.
4. Kojiro was the weapons master to the Daimyo of the Hosokawa clan. Source: ibid
5. Kojiro's retinue comprised body servants, friends, students, cooks, and officials who had come to witness the duel and give report to the daimyo.
Source: ibid
6. Another account recorded that when Kojiro saw Musashi, he drew his sword and threw his scabbard aside. This action made Musashi to taunt him even more by saying: "If you have no more use for your sheath, you are already dead."
Source: Yasuka. "The Duel Between Sasaki Kojirō and Miyamoto Musashi." *KCP International, Japanese Language School*, 26 January 2015.

PART II
WINNING WARS WITHOUT COMBAT

https://libertyanns.medium.com/winning-without-fighting-lessons-from-the-art-of-war-by-sun-tzu-7ac68162831b

https://www.heritage.org/asia/commentary/winning-war-without-fighting

https://www.pambazuka.org/human-security/how-win-war-without-fight

https://www.tm.org/blog/meditation/laozi-and-the-tao-te-ching-the-ancient-wisdom-of-china/

https://hbr.org/2015/12/calming-your-brain-during-conflict

https://blackbeltmag.com/how-to-use-the-combat-concepts-of-legendary-swordsman-miyamoto-musashi-in-21st-century-self-defense

https://davehuer.com/blog/tag/miyamoto-mushashi/

https://cptsdawayout.com/2015/03/20/the-void-the-greatest-samurai-explains-a-devoted-meditator/

https://www.hprc-online.org/mental-fitness/sleep-stress/mindfulness-military

https://www.mindful.org/why-the-army-is-training-in-mindfulness/

https://www.army.mil/article/149615/improving_military_resilience_through_mindfulness_training

https://libertyanns.medium.com/winning-without-fighting-lessons-from-the-art-of-war-by-sun-tzu-7ac68162831b

https://psmag.com/social-justice/a-state-military-mind-42839

http://www.ethikundmilitaer.de/en/full-issues/20192-ethics-for-soldiers/

https://www.militarystrategymagazine.com/article/politics-statecraft-and-the-art-of-war/

https://www.amacad.org/daedalus/ethics-technology-war

https://www.icrc.org/en/doc/assets/files/publications/icrc-0526-002.pdf
https://iep.utm.edu/justwar/
http://isme.tamu.edu/ISME07/Bowyer07.html
https://watson.brown.edu/costsofwar/costs/human
https://watson.brown.edu/costsofwar/costs/human
https://www.e-ir.info/2008/05/22/a-bloodless-war-an-analysis-of-the-weapons-used-by-the-international-campaign-to-ban-landmines/
https://www.peoplesworld.org/article/day-of-the-drone-the-illusion-of-bloodless-war/
https://www.annualreviews.org/doi/pdf/10.1146/annurev-polisci-060314-112706
https://publications.armywarcollege.edu/pubs/2358.pdf
https://www.nytimes.com/1999/01/03/weekinreview/world-war-without-casualties-not-taking-losses-one-thing-winning-another.html

www.ingramcontent.com/pod-product-compliance
Lightning Source LLC
Chambersburg PA
CBHW050111170426
43198CB00014B/2529